P9-CAA-216

Stanley Newman's

CROSSWORD SHORTCUTS

THE

▶▶▶ 1,001 ◀◀◀

MOST COMMON

CROSSWORD

ANSWERS

RANDOM HOUSE PUZZLES & GAMES

NEW YORK   TORONTO   LONDON   SYDNEY   AUCKLAND

Copyright © 2009 by Stanley Newman

All rights reserved. Published in the United States by Random House Puzzles & Games, an imprint of The Random House Information Group, a division of Random House, Inc., New York, and in Canada by Random House of Canada Limited, Toronto.

RANDOM HOUSE is a registered trademark of Random House, Inc.

Please address inquiries about electronic licensing of any products for use on a network, in software or on CD-ROM to the Subsidiary Rights Department, Random House Information Group, fax 212-572-6003.

This book is available at special discounts for bulk purchases for sales promotions or premiums. Special editions, including personalized covers, excerpts of existing books, and corporate imprints, can be created in large quantities for special needs. For more information, write to Random House, Inc., Special Markets/Premium Sales, 1745 Broadway, MD 6-2, New York, NY 10019 or e-mail specialmarkets@randomhouse.com.

Visit the Random House Puzzles & Games Web site: www.randomhouse.com.

Design by Nora Rosansky

Library of Congress Cataloging-in-Publication Data
Newman, Stanley, 1952–
Crossword shortcuts : the 1001 most common crossword answers / Stanley Newman.
p. cm.
ISBN 978-0-375-72306-3
1. Crossword puzzles. I. Title.
GV1507.C7N442   2009
793.73'2—dc22   2008052334

10 9 8 7 6 5 4 3 2 1

ISBN: 978-0-375-72306-3

First Edition

ACKNOWLEDGMENTS

For their help in making this book possible, the author would like to thank:

- Joseph Vallely, my literary agent, for molding my idea into an effective proposal.

- At Random House: Tom Russell, my publisher, and Helena Santini, my editor, for her encouragement and good counsel.

- Kevin McCann, proprietor of the "Crossword Community Center" Web site www.cruciverb.com. Cruciverb includes a database of clues and answers for many of America's best-known crosswords, which I consulted frequently as a check on and a supplement to my own puzzle database and less-than-perfect memory.

Though I've published over 125 books in my "checkered" puzzle career, this is the first one with photographs. You'll find a photo at the beginning of each chapter, representing one of the words to be found within it. It was a new and fascinating experience for me to track these pictures down, made infinitely easier through the Internet. In particular, thanks to the Web site of the U.S. government (www.usa.gov), which has a portal page for public-domain photographs available for download, including those of the Library of Congress, and www.fotolia.com, a "microstock" photo agency, from which I was able to purchase the rights for some photos at a very reasonable price. I'd also like to thank Ken Jennings and Doug Lyons for their help.

And a special thanks to Michael Owen, archivist for the Ira and Leonore Gershwin Trusts, who kindly supplied a photo of Mr. Gershwin, and revealed that Ira was a crossword solver of long standing.

INTRODUCTION

Welcome to *Crossword Shortcuts,* your comprehensive guide to the 1,001 words that appear most often as the answers to American crosswords—the first book of its kind ever published.

As anyone who regularly solves crosswords knows, certain answer words seem to pop up all the time. They're usually three- and four-letter words that are spelled with lots of vowels and common consonants, like ARIA, EAT, and ISLE. As a twenty-five-year veteran of the puzzle biz, as crossword author and editor, I know why this is so.

If you think of a completed crossword diagram as a house, short words with common letters are the necessary "mortar" that makes the longer, more interesting "brick" words in a puzzle possible. In other words, it's simply not possible to create crosswords without using these dependable little words.

The specific 1,001 words that are profiled in *Crossword Shortcuts* were selected based on computer analysis of thousands of recent crosswords from numerous sources, including the puzzles I edit for the Long Island, New York, newspaper *Newsday* and the venerable *New York Times* crossword.

Just how frequently do these 1,001 words appear in crosswords? About 25 percent of the answers in an average weekday themed puzzle will be one of the 1,001. For Sunday puzzles and the tougher, themeless crosswords that often appear in newspapers on Fridays or Saturdays, the percentage is a little lower—about 20 percent or so. That's to be expected, since these tougher-to-make puzzles generally have more longer words.

Clearly then, knowing these words and their meanings is a key for crossword success, perhaps *the* key. If you're just starting out as a crossword solver, *Crossword Shortcuts* will truly live up to its name for you. Under each of the 1,001 words, you'll find the most frequently seen clues for that word, categorized by meaning. For example, the clues for ERA are grouped under its "significant period," "baseball statistic," "Constitutional amendment" and "detergent brand" meanings. If the prospect of learning 1,001 words seems daunting to you, keep in mind that many of these words and their meanings will already be familiar—like ADORE, ERASE, NET, and TAPE.

Even more seasoned solvers will find a lot of good information within these pages. From a list of the world nations that use the PESO, to all the famous people named ANDY from real life and fiction, you're bound to find lots of things to add to your puzzle-solving arsenal.

In addition to the 1,001 words, scattered throughout the book you'll find three special features:

NOT SO FAST! These are common crossword clues that can have two different answers with similar spellings, like "Thin opening," for which SLIT and SLOT are both correct. I've accumulated these "two-way" clues over many years, and hope you'll save yourself a lot of "eraser time" by remembering them.

INSIDER'S TIP: Helpful hints on some of the 1,001 words. For example, ERIE is the only Great Lake spelled with four letters.

SIDEBARS: Groups of words from particular categories, such as "Crossword French 101," and "12 Greek Goddesses You Need to Know."

Your comments on any aspect of this book are most welcome. You can reach me via regular mail at the address below.

If you're Internet-active, you can reach me electronically through my Web site: www.StanXwords.com. StanXwords.com features a new *Newsday* crossword seven days a week, prize contests, puzzlemaker profiles, solving hints, and other fun stuff for crossword fans. Please drop by for a visit.

For a more "hands on" approach to improving your crossword skills, I invite you to join me on my next Crossword University cruise. See below for more info.

Best wishes for crossword success!

Stan Newman
Regular mail: P.O. Box 2, Boca Raton, FL 33497
(Please enclose a self-addressed stamped envelope if you'd like a reply.)

Join Stan Newman on His Annual Crossword University Cruise!

You'll enjoy a relaxing vacation on a luxurious ship, and take your puzzle-solving skills to a whole new level with Stan as your guide. For more info, please phone Special Event Cruises at 1-800-326-0373, or visit their Web site, www.specialeventcruises.com/crossword.html.

FRONT ENTRANCE OF THE ALAMO, SAN ANTONIO, TEXAS, C. 1922.
(*LIBRARY OF CONGRESS*)

the LETTER A

---◀◀◀ **AAA** ▶▶▶---

THE AUTO CLUB

Formerly known as the American Automobile Association, AAA is known for its travel services, such as roadside assistance, maps, and tour books.

THE BOND RATING

AAA is typically the highest rating of creditworthiness that bond-rating services such as Standard & Poor's assign to corporate and municipal bonds.

THE POWER SOURCE

AAA is a standard size of dry-cell batteries, typically used in small electronic devices such as TV remote controls and digital cameras.

THE SHOE WIDTH

Though not commonly seen today, AAA is the narrowest of the standard widths of men's and women's shoes in the United States.

---◀◀◀ **AARON** ▶▶▶---

THE BASEBALL GREAT

At the time of his 1976 retirement, baseball Hall of Famer Henry "Hank" Aaron held many major-league records, including lifetime home runs and runs batted in.

THE BIBLICAL BROTHER

In the Old Testament, Aaron is the older brother of Moses and Miriam. He speaks for Moses in his dealings with the Egyptian royal court, and creates the "golden calf" idol during Moses's long absence on Mount Sinai. He is portrayed in the epic 1956 film *The Ten Commandments* by John Carradine.

THE COMPOSER

The best-known works of Brooklyn-born classical composer Aaron Copland include the ballet scores *Appalachian Spring*, *Billy the Kid*, and *Rodeo*, and "Fanfare for the Common Man."

THE DUELER

Revolutionary War hero and third vice president of the United States (under Jefferson), Aaron Burr is most remembered today for his duel with Alexander Hamilton in 1804.

THE MEDIA MOGUL

TV and film producer Aaron Spelling was responsible for many hit series, including *Charlie's Angels*, *The Love Boat*, and *Dynasty*. His daughter Tori appeared on another of his series, *Beverly Hills 90210*.

--------⟪⟪⟪ **ABA** ⟫⟫⟫--------

THE LAWYERS

ABA is short for the American Bar Association, which sets academic standards for law schools and ethical standards for attorneys.

THE HOOPSTERS

ABA is also short for the American Basketball Association, a professional basketball league founded in the late 1960s. It eventually merged with the NBA (National Basketball Association) in the 1970s.

THE NONSENSE SONG

The 1914 tune "The Aba Daba Honeymoon" concerns an amorous pair of primates. A 1950 recording of the tune by Debbie Reynolds sold over a million copies.

———— <<< **ABATE** >>> ————

THE VERB

Commonly seen clues: "Die down," "Diminish," "Ease off," "Lessen," and "Recede."

———— <<< **ABBA** >>> ————

THE STATESMAN

South African–born Abba Eban was Israel's ambassador to the United Nations and the United States in the 1940s and 1950s, its deputy prime minister in the 1960s, and its foreign minister in the 1960s and 1970s. His books include *Voice of Israel* and *Diplomacy for a New Century.* He is a member of the very exclusive club of celebrities whose first *and* last names are crossword regulars (actor Alan Alda is another).

THE POP GROUP

The 1970s–1980s Swedish music pop quartet ABBA was named for the first letters in the first names of its members. Its hits include "Fernando," "Dancing Queen," and "Waterloo." The Broadway musical *Mamma Mia!* and its 2008 film adaptation are based on the songs of ABBA.

THE RHYME SCHEME

In an ABBA rhyme scheme, the first and fourth lines rhyme, as do the second and third.

---⋘ **ABC** ⋙---

THE NETWORK

Crossword clues for the ABC television network, bought by Disney in 1996, may be as up-to-date as the newest prime-time series. Historically, its most popular series have included *Leave It to Beaver*, *Marcus Welby, M.D.*, *Happy Days*, and *N.Y.P.D. Blue*. More recent shows are *Ugly Betty* and *Grey's Anatomy*.

THE SONG

The 1970 Jackson 5 tune "ABC" reached number 1 on the U.S. Billboard Hot 100 charts.

IT'S SIMPLE

The sense of the clues "Exemplar of simplicity" and "Easy as ___."

---⋘ **ABE** ⋙---

THE PRESIDENT

Nickname of Abraham Lincoln, a.k.a. "Honest Abe," whose portrait can be found on a penny and a $5 bill.

THE TOON

Abe Simpson, Homer's father and Bart's grandfather, is a character on the animated sitcom *The Simpsons*.

THE ACTOR

Abe Vigoda portrayed Detective Sergeant Fish on the sitcom *Barney Miller*.

THE JURIST

Appointed by Lyndon Johnson, Abe Fortas served on the U.S. Supreme Court from 1965 to 1969.

THE PRIME MINISTER

Shinzo Abe served as prime minister of Japan from 2006 to 2007.

THE BROADWAY WRITER/PRODUCER

Abe Burrows was involved with such shows as *Silk Stockings* and *Breakfast at Tiffany's*. He won a Pulitzer Prize for *How to Succeed in Business Without Really Trying*.

--------- <<< **ABEL** >>> ---------

THE SHEPHERD

Abel, son of Adam and Eve, was slain by his brother Cain. Abel's other brother was Seth.

THE EXPLORER

Dutch-born Abel Tasman led the first European expedition to New Zealand and the island named for him, Tasmania, in the 1640s.

THE JUNGLE GUY

Abel is the hero of the W. H. Hudson novel *Green Mansions*, set

Not So Fast!

"Haw partner": H E _

The answer can be either HEM (as in "HEM and HAW") or HEE (as in the HEE-HAW sound of a donkey).

in South America. He is portrayed in the 1959 film adaptation by Anthony Perkins.

⟨⟨⟨ ABET ⟩⟩⟩

THE VERB

Commonly seen clues: "Assist in a crime," "Drive the getaway car," and "Aid partner" (as in the legal phrase "aid and abet").

THE TWO-WORDER

"Not on a bet!" is a colloquial term for "Never!"

⟨⟨⟨ ABLE ⟩⟩⟩

THE ADJECTIVE

Commonly seen clues: "Competent," "Up to the task," "Well-qualified," and "Having the wherewithal."

⟨⟨⟨ ABUT ⟩⟩⟩

THE VERB

Commonly seen clues: "Be adjacent to," "Border on," "Lie next to," "Adjoin," and "Bump up against."

⟨⟨⟨ ACE ⟩⟩⟩

THE SPORTS TERMS

In tennis, an ace is an unreturned serve. In golf, it's a hole-in-one. In baseball, a star player, often a pitcher. In aviation, a hotshot pilot.

THE CARD

The highest-ranking card in a standard deck of fifty-two. In the game blackjack, an ace is worth one point or eleven points.

THE ADJECTIVE AND NOUN

Meaning "expert," in both the adjective and noun senses. Similar clues: "Adept," "Crackerjack," "Champion," and "Top-notch."

<<< **ACHE** >>>

THE NOUN AND VERB

The pain of an ache may be physical or psychological. As in "Yearn," "Feel sore," "Need liniment," "Flu symptom," "Charley horse," and "Feel sympathy for."

<<< **ACID** >>>

THE CHEMICAL

Often clued by example, such as "Boric or acetic." Other acids include amino, hydrochloric, sulfuric, nitric, citric, and folic. In the lab, it's a low-pH chemical that turns blue litmus paper red. An acid's opposite is an alkali, a.k.a. base. It's the "A" in DNA (deoxyribonucleic acid) and RNA (ribonucleic acid). It may also be clued by its practical usage, like "Etcher's chemical" and "Battery fluid."

THE ADJECTIVE

Meaning "sharp" or "biting"—taken literally, as to the taste; figuratively, as criticism.

<<< **ACME** >>>

THE NOUN

Commonly seen clues: "Apex," "Highest point," "Summit," "Zenith," and "Pinnacle."

THE CARTOON CONNECTION

Acme is the mail-order company from which Warner Bros. toon Wile E. Coyote purchases all sorts of outlandish devices in his eternally unsuccessful attempts to do in the Road Runner.

<<< ACRE >>>

THE MEASURE

As a unit of land area, an acre equals 43,560 square feet, or 1/640 of a square mile. Milne bear Winnie-the-Pooh lives in the Hundred Acre Wood. *God's Little Acre* is a novel by Erskine Caldwell.

ON THE MAP

Acre is a city in Israel, near Haifa. It is also the name of a state in the northwest part of Brazil, bordering Bolivia and Peru.

<<< ACT >>>

THE VERB

Commonly seen clues: "Create a role," "Do something," "Perform," "Play a part," and "Take steps." To "act up" is to misbehave.

THE NOUN

An act may be a part of a stage play or opera, a performer's routine, or a pretense. It may also be a piece of legislation or a royal decree.

<<< ADA >>>

THE ABBREVIATIONS

ADA stands for the American Dental Association, whose endorsement can often be seen on boxes of toothpaste. Another or-

ganizational ADA is Americans for Democratic Action, a group
that advocated liberal policies. ADA can also stand for "assistant
district attorney."

THE BOOK

Ada is a 1969 novel by *Lolita* author Vladimir Nabokov.

ON THE MAP

Ada is a city in Oklahoma, as well as a county in Idaho, whose
seat and largest city is Boise.

THE WOMEN

Ada Louise Huxtable is a Pulitzer Prize–winning architecture
critic. Ada Lovelace was a British mathematician and the daughter of Lord Byron. In the movies, characters named Ada are portrayed by Holly Hunter in *The Piano* and Nicole Kidman in *Cold
Mountain*.

————— <<< ADAM >>> —————

FIRST OF ALL

In the book of Genesis, Adam is the husband of Eve, and father
of Cain, Abel, and Seth. The Michelangelo fresco *The Creation
of Adam* is on the ceiling of the Vatican's Sistine Chapel. He's a
character in Milton's *Paradise Lost*.

REAL MEN

There's British economist Smith who wrote *The Wealth of Nations*, actors Sandler, Arkin (son of Alan), and West (TV Batman
of the 1960s), and British rock singer Adam Ant.

UNREAL MEN

Adam is a servant character in Shakespeare's *As You Like It*.

Adam Cartwright is the brother of Joe and Hoss in the TV western series *Bonanza*. Adam Schiff is the district attorney portrayed by Steven Hill in the series *Law & Order*.

——————— <<< **ADD** >>> ———————

THE VERB

Commonly seen clues: "Contribute," "Do sums," "Interject," "Tack on," and "Throw in."

——————— <<< **ADE** >>> ———————

THE DRINK

A soft drink with citrus flavoring, such as lemon, lime, or orange. There's also the brand name Gatorade.

THE WRITER

The best-known work of Indiana-born author/humorist George Ade is *Fables in Slang*.

THE SUFFIX

Besides the citrus fruits, words to which -ADE can be added as a suffix include block, cannon, and chiffon.

——————— <<< **ADELE** >>> ———————

THE PERFORMER

Adele Astaire was the sister of legendary dancer Fred Astaire. Adele and Fred performed together in vaudeville and Broadway, until she retired in the 1930s to marry a British lord.

THE DESIGNER

Adele Simpson was a designer of upscale women's clothing.

THE CHARACTERS

The Story of Adele H. is a 1975 film directed by François Truffaut. Adele is the maid character in the Johann Strauss opera *Die Fledermaus*, and one of the pupils of the title character in the Charlotte Brontë novel *Jane Eyre*.

 **ADEN**

ON THE MAP

Aden is a seaport and former capital of the Mideast nation of Yemen, located on the Gulf of Aden.

ADIEU

THE PARTING WORD

Commonly seen clues: "French farewell," "Good-bye," and "It may be bid" (as in to "bid adieu").

ADO

THE FUSS

Commonly seen clues: "Commotion," "Excitement," "Hoo-ha," "Hoopla," "Hubbub," and "Ruckus."

ON THE STAGE

Ado Annie is a character in the Rodgers and Hammerstein musical *Oklahoma!* And let us not forget the Shakespeare comedy *Much Ado About Nothing*.

 **ADORE**

THE VERB

Commonly seen clues: "Be gaga over," "Cherish," "Hold dear," "Like a lot," "Love," "Venerate," and "Worship."

<<< **AERIE** >>>

ON HIGH

An aerie is the lofty nest of a bird of prey, such as an eagle or hawk. It can also be a house or fortress located high on a mountain.

<<< **AERO** >>>

THE ADJECTIVE

It can mean "pertaining to aircraft" and is also a shortened form of "aerodynamic," especially when it pertains to the design of a vehicle.

THE PREFIX

In addition to "dynamic," AERO- can precede words such as ballistic, biology, marine, nautical, and space.

THE PROPER NAMES

Aero is the graphical user interface of the Windows Vista computer operating system. The Akron Aeros are a minor-league baseball team.

<<< **AFAR** >>>

THE ADVERB

Commonly seen clues: "In the distance," "Miles away," "Way off," "Worship from __," and "Yonder."

<<< **AFRO** >>>

THE HAIR

The spherical hairstyle popular in the 1960s and 1970s was worn by African Americans such as Jesse Jackson and Jimi Hendrix.

◀◀◀ **AGA** ▶▶▶

THE TITLE

In Turkey and other Muslim countries, it is a title of respect; or the title for a general. Aga Khan is the hereditary title of the leader of a Muslim sect.

◀◀◀ **AGAIN** ▶▶▶

THE ADVERB

Commonly seen clues: "Another time," "From the top," and "Once more." It is also the last word of the "Humpty Dumpty" nursery rhyme.

◀◀◀ **AGAR** ▶▶▶

THE EDIBLE

Agar is used as a gelatin substitute, in the laboratory as a culture medium, and as a thickening agent in foods such as ice creams and soups.

THE MAN

Actor John Agar was the first husband of actress Shirley Temple. He appeared in such films as *Fort Apache* and *Sands of Iwo Jima*.

◀◀◀ **AGE** ▶▶▶

THE VERB

Commonly seen clues: "Get older," "Improve, as wine," "Mature," "Mellow," and "Ripen."

THE NOUN

Commonly seen clues: "Candle count" (as in birthday candles),

"Era," "Generation," "Historical period," "Retirement factor," and "Time of one's life."

⟨⟨⟨ AGEE ⟩⟩⟩

THE WRITER

James Agee was a cowriter of the screenplay for the Humphrey Bogart film *The African Queen* and the film critic for *Time* magazine in the 1940s, and he received a posthumous Pulitzer Prize in 1958.

THE BASEBALL PLAYER

Center fielder Tommie Agee was a key player in the New York Mets "miracle" 1969 season, including its World Series triumph.

⟨⟨⟨ AGENT ⟩⟩⟩

IN GENERAL

Commonly seen clues: "Actor's representative," "Contract negotiator," "FBI employee," "Go-between," "Intermediary," and "Operative."

SPECIFICALLY

Fictional agents often seen in "clues by example" include James Bond (a.k.a. 007), Mulder and Scully from the TV series *The X-Files*, Austin Powers (portrayed by Mike Myers in films), Maxwell Smart (portrayed by Don Adams on TV and Steve Carell in a 2008 film), and the John le Carré novel character George Smiley.

⟨⟨⟨ AGER ⟩⟩⟩

THE THINGS

Commonly seen clues: "Antiquing agent," "Maturing agent," and "Stress, it's said."

THE PEOPLE

Composer Milton Ager wrote such songs as "Ain't She Sweet?" and "Happy Days Are Here Again." A "Golden Ager" is a senior citizen, and the clue "Teen follower" indicates the "ager" part of "teenager."

———— <<< **AGO** >>> ————

THE ADJECTIVE

Commonly seen clues: "Back in time," "Gone by," "In the past," "Long, long __," "Many moons __," and "Years __."

THE TWO-WORDER

"Give it __" and "Have __ at," both colloquial terms for "try," are common clues for A Go.

———— <<< **AGRA** >>> ————

ON THE MAP

This city in the Uttar Pradesh state of northern India, on the Yamuna River, is most famous as the site of the Taj Mahal. The Pearl Mosque is another popular tourist attraction in the city. Agra was the capital of the Mogul Empire in the sixteenth and seventeenth centuries.

———— <<< **AGREE** >>> ————

THE VERB

Commonly seen clues: "Coincide," "Come to terms," "Concur," "Go along," "Match," "See eye to eye," and "Think alike."

─────◄◄◄ **AHA** ►►►─────

THE EXCLAMATION

Commonly seen clues: "Cry of discovery," "Eureka!," "Gotcha!," "I understand now!," and "So that's it!" OHO is very similar in meaning and has many of the same clues.

THE ROCK GROUP

The Norwegian rock band a-ha had a number 1 tune in 1985 with "Take on Me."

─────◄◄◄ **AHAB** ►►►─────

IN LITERATURE

The obsessed Captain Ahab is the skipper of the whaler *Pequod* in the Herman Melville novel *Moby-Dick*. His subordinates include Ishmael, Queequeg, and Starbuck. Ahab was portrayed by Gregory Peck in the 1956 film adaptation.

IN THE BIBLE

In the Old Testament, Ahab is a king of ancient Israel. He is the son and successor of Omri and the husband of Jezebel.

IN SONG

"Ahab the Arab" is a 1962 novelty song by Ray Stevens.

─────◄◄◄ **AHEM** ►►►─────

THE EXCLAMATION

Commonly seen clues: "Attention-getter," "Excuse me!," "I beg your pardon," and "Throat-clearing sound."

─── <<< **AIDA** >>> ───

THE OPERA

Aida is the title character in the opera of the same name by Giuseppe Verdi. She is an Ethiopian princess who is captured and brought into slavery in Egypt. Her love is Radames, captain of the guard. A 1953 Italian film adaptation stars Sophia Loren in the title role.

THE PLAY

The Disney-produced musical drama based on the opera, with music by Elton John and lyrics by Tim Rice, had a 2000–2004 run on Broadway.

THE ACTRESS

Aida Turturro, cousin of John, portrayed Janice Soprano (sister of Tony) in the HBO series *The Sopranos.*

─── <<< **AIDE** >>> ───

THE HELPER

Commonly seen clues: "Assistant," "Deputy," "Gofer," "Right-hand person," "Subordinate," and "White House worker."

─── <<< **AIL** >>> ───

THE VERB

Commonly seen clues: "Be under the weather," "Feel poorly," "Have a bug," and other very similar colloquial synonyms.

─── <<< **AIM** >>> ───

THE VERB

Commonly seen verb clues: "Draw a bead," "Point at the target,"

Not So Fast!

"Less cooked": R A _ E R

The answer can be either RAWER (food in general) or RARER (steak in particular).

"Set one's sights," "Prepare to shoot," and "We __ to please." Referring to "Ready, aim, fire," you may also see "Ready follower" and "Fire preceder."

THE NOUN

Commonly seen noun clues: "Ambition," "Goal," "Intention," "Purpose," and "Sharpshooter's asset."

THE TOOTHPASTE BRAND

In this sense, usually clued in terms of its competitors, which include Close-Up, Colgate, Crest, and Gleem.

——— <<< **AINT** >>> ———

BLANKETY-BLANKS

Commonly seen colloquialisms include: "If it __ broke . . . ," "It __ over till it's over," "__ it the truth," and "Say it __ so."

BLANKLESS

Commonly seen clues: "Isn't, informally" and "Nonstandard contraction."

IN SONGS

Popular song titles that include the word: "Ain't Misbehavin',"

"Ain't No Sunshine," "Ain't She Sweet," "Ain't That a Shame," "Ain't We Got Fun," and "It Ain't Necessarily So."

‹‹‹ AIR ›››

THE NOUN

Commonly seen atmospheric clues: "Balloon filler," "Football filler," "Former gas-station freebie," and "Vacuum's lack." The word may also refer to the appearance and bearing of a person as well as a melody.

THE VERB

Commonly seen clues: "Broadcast," "Expose," "Publicize," "Televise," and "Ventilate."

‹‹‹ AISLE ›››

THE NOUN

The aisles seen in crosswords are usually in airplanes, churches, supermarkets, or theaters. Other related clues: "Narrow walkway," "Seat selection," and "Usher's domain."

‹‹‹ AJAR ›››

THE ADJECTIVE/ADVERB

Commonly seen clues: "Admitting a draft," "Barely open," "Not quite shut," and "Open a crack."

‹‹‹ AKA ›››

THE ABBREVIATION

Standing for "also known as," commonly seen clues include "Alias: Abbr.," "Rap-sheet letters," "Sometimes called," and "Wanted poster initials."

⟨⟨⟨ **AKIN** ⟩⟩⟩

THE ADJECTIVE

Commonly seen clues: "Analogous," "Comparable," "Related," and "Similar."

⟨⟨⟨ **ALA** ⟩⟩⟩

ON THE MAP

As an abbreviation for Alabama, it'll be worth your while to know the state's nickname ("Heart of Dixie"), neighbors (Florida, Georgia, Mississippi, and Tennessee), major cities (Birmingham, Huntsville, Mobile, Montgomery, and Tuscaloosa), and universities (Auburn, Tuskegee, and the University of Alabama, whose sports teams are known as the Crimson Tide).

ON THE MENU

The two-word A LA means "like" or "in the style of," as in the menu phrases "à la carte," "Chicken à la king," and "Pie à la mode."

⟨⟨⟨ **ALAI** ⟩⟩⟩

THE GAME

Nearly always clued these days as "Jai ___." The game of jai alai, literally "merry festival" in the Basque language, originated in Spain. Similar to handball, it is played on a court called a "fronton." Players catch and propel the ball with a basketlike device called a "cesta."

ON THE MAP

When not part of the game, Alai is a mountain range located in Kyrgyzstan and Tajikistan.

——— <<< **ALAMO** >>> ———

THE SHRINE

This San Antonio museum, once a mission, was the site of the 1836 battle between the forces of the Republic of Texas (which included Jim Bowie and Davy Crockett) and Mexico (led by Santa Anna).

THE RENT-A-CAR COMPANY

In this sense, usually clued in terms of its competitors, which include Avis, Budget, Dollar, Hertz, and National.

——— <<< **ALAN** >>> ———

THE ASTRONAUTS

Alan Shepard was the first American in space, and later commanded the Apollo 14 mission to the moon. Alan Bean was the fourth man to walk on the moon.

IN ENTERTAINMENT

There's Alda (of *M*A*S*H*), Arkin (Oscar winner for *Little Miss Sunshine*), Ayckbourn (knighted British playwright), Bates (knighted British actor), Freed (pioneering rock-and-roll DJ), Hale (of *Gilligan's Island*), King (comedian), Ladd (of *Shane*), Paton (South African author), Rickman (the villain in *Die Hard*), Thicke (of *Growing Pains*), and Young (of *Mister Ed*). Lyricist Alan Jay Lerner collaborated with Frederick Loewe on many memorable musicals.

IN GOVERNMENT

Chester Alan Arthur was the twenty-first president of the United

States. Economist Alan Greenspan served as head of the Federal Reserve from 1987 to 2006.

<<< **ALAR** >>>

THE BRAND NAME

A chemical once sprayed on fruit to regulate its growth, Alar was banned by the EPA in 1989.

THE ADJECTIVE

In uncapitalized form, it means "winglike," from the Latin word for "wing."

<<< **ALAS** >>>

THE EXCLAMATION

Commonly seen clues: "So sorry!," "Too bad!," "Woe is me!," and "Word of regret." Hamlet says "Alas, poor Yorick . . ." in Shakespeare's play.

<<< **ALDA** >>>

THE SON

By virtue of his conveniently spelled first and last names, Alan Alda is the crossword world's Most Valuable Person. Best known for his starring role as Hawkeye Pierce in the sitcom *M*A*S*H*, his other TV credits include *Scientific American Frontiers* and *The West Wing*. He has directed such films as *Betsy's Wedding* and *The Four Seasons*.

THE DAD

Alan's father Robert originated the role of Sky Masterson in the musical *Guys and Dolls* and portrayed George Gershwin in the 1945 biopic *Rhapsody in Blue*.

———— <<< **ALE** >>> ————

THE DRINK

Commonly seen clues: "British brew," "Pub serving," "Stein filler," and "Stout relative" (stout is a malt beverage). Popular brands of ale include Ballantine, Bass, Guinness, and McSorley's. *Cakes and Ale* is a novel by Somerset Maugham. And of course, there's the nonalcoholic ginger ale.

———— <<< **ALEC** >>> ————

THE AMERICAN

Actor Alec Baldwin has appeared in many films, plus the sitcom *30 Rock*. His acting brothers are Daniel, Stephen, and William. He was formerly married to actress Kim Basinger.

THE BRITS

Actor Sir Alec Guinness portrays Obi-Wan Kenobi in the film *Star Wars*. Sir Alec Douglas-Home (pronounced "Hume") served as British prime minister in the 1960s. Novelist Alec Waugh was the elder brother of novelist Evelyn Waugh. Pianist Alec Templeton had his own U.S. radio show in the 1940s.

———— <<< **ALEE** >>> ————

AT SEA

A nautical term meaning "toward the lee (sheltered) side of a vessel" or "away from the wind." It is the opposite of "aweather" or "windward." A captain might give the order "Hard alee!"

⫸⫷ ALERT ⫸⫷

THE ADJECTIVE

Commonly seen adjective clues: "Attentive," "On one's toes," "Vigilant," "Watchful," and "Wide awake."

THE VERB

Commonly seen verb clues: "Give notice to," "Tip off," and "Warn."

THE NOUN

Commonly seen noun clues: "Heads-up," "Siren, for example," and "State of readiness."

⫸⫷ ALEX ⫸⫷

THE EMCEE

Alex Trebek has been the host of the game show *Jeopardy!* since 1984.

THE AUTHOR

Alex Haley wrote the 1970s best seller *Roots*.

ON THE FIELD

Baseball star Alex Rodriguez is known by the nickname A-Rod. Former pro footballer Alex Karras became an actor after his playing career.

THE TV ROLES

Michael J. Fox portrayed Alex Keaton on the sitcom *Family Ties*. Judd Hirsch portrayed Alex Reiger on the sitcom *Taxi*. Swoosie Kurtz portrayed Alex Barber on the series *Sisters*.

Not So Fast!

"Coke product": T A _

*The answer can be TAB (a diet soft drink made by Coca-Cola),
or TAR (which can be made from coke, the solid obtained by
distilling coal).*

<<< **ALI** >>>

THE BOXER

Born Cassius Clay, Muhammad Ali was world heavyweight boxing champ for three separate periods in the 1960s and 1970s. Nicknamed "The Greatest," Ali was named "Sportsman of the Century" by *Sports Illustrated* in 1999. His daughter Laila Ali is also a professional boxer. Will Smith portrays him in the 2001 biopic *Ali*.

THE WOODCUTTER

Ali Baba is the poor woodcutter who outwits the Forty Thieves in the *Arabian Nights* tale.

THE ACTRESSES

Former fashion model Ali (short for Alison) Larter is a star of the sci-fi TV series *Heroes*. Ali (short for Alice) MacGraw is best known for her Oscar-nominated role in the 1970 film *Love Story*.

<<< **ALIE** >>>

BLANKETY-BLANKS

Clues almost always involve either "I cannot tell a lie" (what

George Washington didn't say), the 1930s song "It's a Sin to Tell a Lie," or the colloquial denial "That's a lie!"

<<< ALIEN >>>

FROM ANOTHER COUNTRY

Commonly seen clues: "Foreigner," "Green-card holder," and "Non-native."

FROM ANOTHER PLANET

Commonly seen clues: "Extraterrestrial," "Martian," "Superman," and "UFO pilot." The 1979 film *Alien* stars Sigourney Weaver.

THE ADJECTIVE

Commonly seen clues: "Otherworldly," "Strange," and "Unfamiliar."

<<< ALIT >>>

THE VERB

The past tense of "alight." Commonly seen clues: "Dismounted," "Got off," "Landed," "Returned to Earth," "Stepped off," and "Touched down."

<<< ALIVE >>>

THE ADJECTIVE

Commonly seen clues: "Animated," "Full of energy," "Still in the game," and "Vibrant."

THE PARTNERS

The clues "Kicking partner" and "Well partner" refer to the phrases "alive and kicking" and "alive and well."

<<< ALL >>>

THE ADJECTIVE

Commonly seen clues: "100%," "Completely," "Everyone," "Nothing but," "Solely," and "Totally."

THE DETERGENT

In this sense, usually clued in terms of its competitors, which include Era, Fab, Surf, Tide, and Wisk.

<<< ALMA >>>

SCHOOL DAYS

Your alma mater may be the school that you graduated from, as well as the official anthem of that school. The phrase is Latin for "nurturing mother."

ON THE MAP

Alma-Ata is the former name of the largest city in Kazakhstan, which is known today as Almaty.

THE SINGER

Soprano Alma Gluck was one of the world's most famous singers about a hundred years ago. She was the mother of actor Efrem Zimbalist Jr.

<<< ALOE >>>

THE PLANT AND ITS USES

Native to Africa, aloes are succulent plants often seen in gardens and on windowsills. The most popular of the hundreds of species is aloe vera. The gel from its leaves is used as an emollient (soother), and is often an ingredient in skin creams, moisturizers, and other lotions.

─────── <<< **ALOHA** >>> ───────

ON THE ISLANDS

In Hawaiian, the word can mean "hello" or "good-bye." The NFL's annual post-season Pro Bowl is held annually at Hawaii's Aloha Stadium. Honolulu-based Aloha Airlines handles cargo only, having ceased passenger service in 2008.

─────── <<< **ALONE** >>> ───────

THE ADJECTIVE

Commonly seen clues: "By oneself," "Isolated," "Solo," "Stag," "Unassisted," and "Unaccompanied."

─────── <<< **ALOU** >>> ───────

ON THE DIAMOND

Four members of the Dominican-born Alou family have played in the major leagues: Felipe, his brothers Jesus and Matty, and Felipe's son Moisés.

─────── <<< **ALS** >>> ───────

THE ACTORS

The most famous acting Al is Oscar-winner Pacino. Others are Franken (*Saturday Night Live*) and Molinaro (*Happy Days*).

IN SPORTS

Al Unser and his son Al Junior both won the Indianapolis 500 auto race. Baseball Hall of Famer Al Kaline played his entire career with the Detroit Tigers. Al Oerter was a four-time Olympic champion in the discus.

IN MUSIC

Singing Als include Green, Jarreau, Jolson, Martino, and parodist "Weird Al" Yankovic. Al Hirt was a Dixieland trumpeter.

IN POLITICS

Former vice president Al Gore shared the 2007 Nobel Peace Prize. Al Haig served as secretary of state under Ronald Reagan. New York governor Al Smith was the unsuccessful Democratic presidential candidate in 1928, losing to Herbert Hoover. Al D'Amato is a former U.S. senator from New York. Baptist minister Al Sharpton is best known as a political activist.

OTHER CELEBS

Cartoonist Al Capp was best known for his *L'il Abner* strip. The infamous Al Capone was a crime-syndicate leader during the Prohibition era. Al Hirschfeld was a show-biz caricaturist for over seventy years.

———— <<< **ALSO** >>> ————

THE ADVERB

Commonly seen clues: "Additionally," "As well," "Furthermore," "In addition," "Likewise," "Moreover," "Plus," and "Too."

———— <<< **ALT** >>> ————

THE ABBREVIATIONS

"Substitute: Abbr." clues the shortened form of "alternate." "Hgt." and "Cockpit abbr." indicate the shortened form of "altitude."

THE KEY
The computer-keyboard Alt key is usually located in the bottom row, adjacent to the space bar.

THE MODEL
Supermodel Carol Alt appeared on over 500 magazine covers in the 1980s.

———⫷⫷⫷ **ALTAR** ⫸⫸⫸———

THE RELIGIOUS PLACE
Commonly seen clues: "Church platform," "Rite place," "Vow venue," and "Wedding site."

———⫷⫷⫷ **ALTER** ⫸⫸⫸———

THE VERB
Commonly seen clues: "Adjust," "Amend," "Change," "Modify," "Refit," and "Transform." The clues "Rehem" and "Take in or let out" relate specifically to tailoring.

———⫷⫷⫷ **ALTO** ⫸⫸⫸———

MUSICALLY SPEAKING
The alto female-voice range is lower than soprano, but higher than tenor. It is also the range of some musical instruments, such as the saxophone and flute.

ON THE MAP
Palo Alto, literally "high stick" in Spanish, is located in California's Silicon Valley, and is the headquarters of computer manufacturer Hewlett-Packard.

Need to Know: Crossword French 101

The 30 French words that appear most often as crossword answers (accent and diacritical marks, if any, are omitted):

adieu (good-bye)

ami (male friend, amie is female friend)

bon (good)

eau (water)

entre (between)

est (is)

etat (state)

ete (summer)

etes (are, summers)

etre (to be)

ici (here)

idee (idea)

ile (island)

lait (milk)

les (the)

mer (sea)

Mlle. (Miss or Ms.)

Mme. (Mrs.)

mon (my)

mot (word)

nee (born)

noir (black)

oui (yes)

pere (father)

roi (king)

sel (salt)

ste. (female saint)

tete (head)

tres (very)

une (one)

─── <<< **ALUM** >>> ───

OUT OF SCHOOL

As a short form of "alumnus," commonly seen clues include: "Grad," "Homecoming attendee," and "Reunion goer."

IN THE MEDICINE CHEST

This alum, known chemically as aluminum potassium sulfate, is an astringent (tissue-contracting agent), often used in styptic pencils to stop the bleeding from minor cuts.

─── <<< **AMA** >>> ───

THE DOC BLOC

As an abbreviation for American Medical Association, commonly seen clues are usually variations of "Drs.' org." and "Physicians' grp."

THE TITLES

"I Am a Rock" is a 1960s song popularized by Simon and Garfunkel. *I Am a Camera* is a 1955 film based on the Christopher Isherwood novel *Goodbye to Berlin,* which was also the source for the musical play and film *Cabaret.*

─── <<< **AMASS** >>> ───

THE VERB

Commonly seen clues: "Accumulate," "Collect," "Gather," and "Pile up."

─── <<< **AMATI** >>> ───

THE CRAFTSMEN AND THEIR CREATIONS

The Amati family, natives of Cremona, Italy, were violinmakers from the sixteenth to eighteenth centuries. Antonio Stradivari learned his craft from one of the Amatis. An "Amati" is also any violin manufactured by one of the Amatis.

<<< **AMEN** >>>

RELIGIOUSLY SPEAKING

Commonly seen clues: "Grace finale," "Hymn ending," and "Prayer conclusion." It is the last word of the New Testament.

THE SECULAR EXCLAMATION

As an expression of agreement, AMEN is usually clued colloquially with variations on "I agree!," "Right on!," and "You said it!"

ON TV

The sitcom *Amen* ran from 1986 to 1991, starring Sherman Hemsley as a Philadelphia deacon.

<<< **AMES** >>>

ON THE MAP

The city of Ames, on the Skunk River, is the home of Iowa State University.

Not So Fast!

"Get away from": E _ _ D E

The answer can be EVADE as well as the nearly synonymous ELUDE.

THE SURNAME

In the 1960s, Ed Ames appeared on the TV series *Daniel Boone* and had a top-10 song, "My Cup Runneth Over." Aldrich Ames was a former CIA agent convicted in 1994 of spying for Russia.

———— <<< **AMI** >>> ————

IN FRENCH

As the French word for "friend," commonly seen clues are variations of "Buddy in Bordeaux" and "Parisian pal."

BLANKETY-BLANKS

Cluing the two words AM I, commonly seen colloquialisms include "What __, chopped liver?" and "Who __ to argue?" From Genesis, there's "__ my brother's keeper?" And let's not forget the immortal words of Little Jack Horner, "What a good boy __."

———— <<< **AMID** >>> ————

THE PREPOSITION

Commonly seen clues: "During," "In the center of," and "Surrounded by."

———— <<< **AMMO** >>> ————

IN WEAPONS

As the short form of "ammunition," commonly seen clues include "Arsenal contents," "Bullets," "Military stockpile," and "Sharpshooter's need."

─────── <<< **AMO** >>> ───────

FOR LOVERS

Amo means "I love" in Latin and Spanish.

─────── <<< **AMOK** >>> ───────

THE ADVERB

Commonly seen clues: "In a frenzy," "Out of control," "Run __," and "Wildly."

─────── <<< **AMOR** >>> ───────

FOR LOVERS

Amor is the word for "love" in Latin and Spanish. Amor was another name for the Roman love god Cupid, the son of Venus. The Latin expression *"Omnia vincit amor"* means "Love conquers all."

─────── <<< **AMOS** >>> ───────

IN THE BIBLE

Amos is a book of the Old Testament, named for a Minor Prophet.

LAST NAMES

Tori Amos is a pop singer/pianist. Actor John Amos appeared in the miniseries *Roots* and was a regular on the 1970s sitcom *Good Times*. Cookie entrepreneur Wally Amos gave his name to the Famous Amos brand.

FIRST NAMES

Amos Oz is an Israeli author. Amos Alonzo Stagg had a fifty-six-year career as a college football coach. *Amos 'n' Andy* was a long-running sitcom on old-time radio.

⏪ AMP ⏩

IN PHYSICS

Short for "ampere," the amp is a unit of current.

IN SOUND

As a shortened form of "amplifier," commonly seen clues include: "Guitarist gear," "Rock-concert equipment," "Sound booster," and "Stereo component."

⏪ ANA ⏩

THE SANTAS

Santa Ana, California, is the largest city in Orange County. Santa Ana winds sweep through southern California in late fall and winter.

THE PEOPLE

Ana Ivanovic is a tennis pro from Serbia, Ana Gasteyer was once a regular on *Saturday Night Live,* and actress Ana-Alicia is best known for her starring role in the TV series *Falcon Crest.*

IN THE AIR

ANA, short for All Nippon Airways, is Japan's second largest international airline.

IN THE DICTIONARY

An ana is a collection of miscellaneous information on a particular subject.

COLLOQUIALLY

As in the phrase "Get an A for effort."

INSIDER'S TIP: *Be careful on this last one, because "Get an E for effort" is also a common phrase, so the answer to "Get ___ for effort" may be either AN A or AN E.*

------------ <<< **ANAT** >>> ------------

THE ABBREVIATION
Short for "anatomy," commonly seen clues are generally variations of "Med. school class" and "Gray's subj." (Henry Gray's anatomy textbook, first published in 1858, is still in print, now in its thirty-ninth edition.)

------------ <<< **AND** >>> ------------

THE CONJUNCTION
Commonly seen clues: "As well as," "Furthermore," "In addition," "Moreover," and "Plus."

------------ <<< **ANDY** >>> ------------

IN SPORTS
Andy Pettitte is a major-league pitcher, Andy Roddick is a tennis pro, and Andy Granatelli is a retired race-car driver.

ON TV
Andy Rooney is the longtime commentator for *60 Minutes*, and Andy Griffith portrayed the sheriff of Mayberry and father of Opie on *The Andy Griffith Show*.

OTHER CELEBRITIES
There's film actor Andy Garcia, pop singer Andy Gibb, pop artist Andy Warhol, and singer Andy Williams.

IN FICTION

Andy is the steamboat captain in Edna Ferber's *Show Boat* and the musical based on it, and Andy is the boy who owns the toys in the *Toy Story* series of animated films. Rag doll Raggedy Andy is the brother of Raggedy Ann in a series of children's books.

<<< **ANE** >>>

ON TV

The clue "*Wheel of Fortune* purchase" refers to the $250 cost of buying any vowel, an "E" in particular. While AN A, AN I, and AN O are also possible answers, AN E is by far the one most frequently seen (with AN I a distant second).

IN THE LAB

In chemistry, -ane is a suffix for hydrocarbon compounds, such as methane and butane.

THE ACTRESS

Sue Ane Langdon appeared in two Elvis Presley films of the 1960s.

COLLOQUIALLY

As in the phrase "Get an A for effort."

INSIDER'S TIP: Be careful on this last one, because "Get an A for effort" is also a common phrase, so the answer to "Get ___ for effort" may be either AN E or AN A.

<<< **ANEAR** >>>

THE ADVERB

"Anear" is an old-style/poetic form of "near."

COLLOQUIALLY SPEAKING

To "lend an ear" is to listen carefully, and to "keep an ear to the ground" is to look out for new information.

<<< **ANEW** >>>

THE ADVERB

Commonly seen clues: "All over again," "Another time," "From scratch," "From the top," and "Once more."

<<< **ANI** >>>

ON TV

The clue "*Wheel of Fortune* purchase" refers to the $250 cost of buying any vowel, an "I" in particular. AN A, AN E, and AN O are also possible answers; AN E is by far the one most frequently seen (with AN I a distant second).

IN THE AIR

An ani is a black, tropical American cuckoo. It is an endangered species in crosswords, because of contemporary editors' distaste for words seldom seen outside of puzzles.

Not So Fast!

"Bird home": C _ _ E

The answer can be CAGE (at home or in zoos) as well as COTE (as in pigeons or doves).

THE NAME

Ani DiFranco is a folk-rock singer. Ani is also the nickname for young Anakin Skywalker, father of Luke Skywalker, in the *Star Wars* film series.

<<< ANITA >>>

THE SINGERS

There's soul singer Anita Baker, pop singer Anita Bryant, and jazz singer Anita O'Day.

OTHER CELEBRITIES

Writer Anita Loos is best known for *Gentlemen Prefer Blondes*. Actress Anita Ekberg starred in the Fellini film *La Dolce Vita*, and Anita Gillette is known for her Broadway roles and game-show appearances.

<<< ANKA >>>

THE SINGER/SONGWRITER

The song hits of Canadian-born Paul Anka include "Diana," "Times of Your Life," "Puppy Love," and "My Way." He composed "Johnny's Theme," the theme music for *The Tonight Show* when Johnny Carson was the host.

<<< ANN >>>

IN THE MOVIES

There's actresses Blyth, Jillian, Miller, Reinking, Sheridan, and Sothern. Ann Darrow is the female role in the original *King Kong* film (portrayed by Fay Wray) and the 2005 remake (portrayed by Naomi Watts).

OTHER CELEBRITIES

Writers named Ann include Beattie, Coulter, Patchett, and Rule. Ann Compton and Ann Curry are TV journalists. Ann Lee founded the Shakers religious sect. Advice columnist Ann Landers was the twin sister of advice columnist Dear Abby. Ann Richards was governor of Texas in the 1990s.

UNREAL ANNS

Ann Taylor is the name of a chain of women's clothing stores, but the name was made up and isn't the name of a real person. Rag doll Raggedy Ann is the sister of Raggedy Andy in a series of children's books.

ANN IN THE MIDDLE

Lee Ann Womack is a country singer, Penelope Ann Miller is an actress, Mary Ann Evans was the real name of British writer George Eliot, and "Barbara Ann" is a Beach Boys tune.

ON THE MAP

Ann Arbor, Michigan, is near Detroit. Cape Ann is in eastern Massachusetts.

————— <<< **ANNA** >>> —————

FOR REAL

Authors named Anna include Sewell and Quindlen. Actress Annas include Faris, Magnani, and Paquin. First Lady Eleanor Roosevelt's full name was Anna Eleanor Roosevelt. Anna Kournikova is a Russian tennis pro. Anna Pavlova was a Russian ballerina. Anna Moffo was a Russian-born opera star. Anna Freud, daughter of psychologist Sigmund, was also a psychologist.

IN FICTION

She's the title character in Eugene O'Neill's play *Anna Christie,* the Tolstoy novel *Anna Karenina,* and the "I" in the Rodgers and Hammerstein musical *The King and I.*

———— <<< **ANNE** >>> ————

WRITERS AND WRITINGS

Anne Frank wrote a famous World War II–era diary. Anne Brontë was the sister of Charlotte and Emily. Anne Rice is best known for her vampire novels, Anne Tyler for *The Accidental Tourist.* *Anne of Green Gables* is a novel by Canadian author Lucy Maud Montgomery.

THE ACTRESSES

There's Archer, Bancroft, Baxter, Francis, Hathaway, Heche, Jackson, and Meara (mother of actor Ben Stiller).

THE BRITS

Princess Anne is the daughter of Queen Elizabeth II. Queen Anne succeeded her father James II to the throne of England in 1702, and two of Henry VIII's six wives were Annes: Anne Boleyn and Anne of Cleves. Anne was the name of William Shakespeare's wife.

OTHER CELEBRITIES

Anne Klein is a fashion designer, and Anne Murray is a Canadian-born pop singer.

———— <<< **ANNIE** >>> ————

FOR REAL

The life of sharpshooter Annie Oakley was the basis of the musical *Annie Get Your Gun*. There's also singer Lennox, photographer Leibovitz, and actress Potts.

IN FICTION

The comic strip *Little Orphan Annie* was turned into the musical *Annie*, in which the title character sings "Tomorrow." Annie's dog is named Sandy and her guardian is Daddy Warbucks. The title character in the Woody Allen film *Annie Hall* was portrayed by Diane Keaton.

<<< ANODE >>>

IN PHYSICS

An anode is the negative terminal (or electrode) of a battery, or the positive terminal of an electron tube. In both senses, it's the opposite of a cathode.

<<< ANON >>>

THE ABBREVIATION

As a short form of "anonymous," commonly seen clues include variations of "Quote-book abbr." and "Unknown auth."

THE ADVERB

As a synonym for "soon," often seen in poems, commonly seen clues include "Before long," "In a while," "Presently," and "Shortly, to Shakespeare."

<<< ANS >>>

THE ABBREVIATION

As a short form of "answer," commonly seen clues include "Part of Q&A," "Reply: Abbr.," "Response: Abbr.," "RSVP, e.g.," and "Solution: Abbr."

<<< **ANT** >>>

THE INSECT

Commonly seen clues: "Aardvark snack," "Hill builder," "Pantry invader," "Picnic pest," and "Tiny colonist."

<<< **ANTE** >>>

CARDWISE

In the sense of an initial payment in poker, commonly seen clues include: "Chip in a chip," "Deal preceder," "Pay to play," "Penny, perhaps," and "Start the pot."

FROM THE LATIN

Ante is the Latin word for "before," and the "a" in the timely abbreviation "a.m."

<<< **ANTI** >>>

FOR STARTERS

As a prefix meaning "against," commonly seen clues include "Contra- relative," "Part of ABM" (as in "antiballistic missile"), and clues that start with "Prefix for" and usually end with "freeze," "social," or "virus."

THE NOUN

In the sense of a person who is against something, commonly seen clues include "Dissenter," "Naysayer," "Opponent," and "Pro foe."

<<< **ANY** >>>

THE ADJECTIVE

Commonly seen clues: "Even one," "One or more," and "Whichever."

IN TITLES

"Any" films include *Any Given Sunday* (directed by Oliver Stone), *Any Wednesday* (starring Jane Fonda and Jason Robards), and *Any Which Way You Can* (with Clint Eastwood). *Unsafe at Any Speed* is Ralph Nader's book on auto safety.

OTHER BLANKETY-BLANKS

Common colloquialism clues: "__ luck?," "__ objections?," and "__ takers?" There's also the excerpt from the "Baa Baa Black Sheep" nursery rhyme, "Have you __ wool?"

<<< **AOK** >>>

GREAT STUFF

Correctly spelled "A-OK," it means "okay" or "perfect," often associated with space flights. Commonly seen clues are variations of "Hunky-dory," "Just fine," and "NASA affirmative."

<<< **AONE** >>>

GREAT STUFF

Commonly seen clues: "Excellent," "First-class," "Superb," and "Top-notch."

<<< **AORTA** >>>

HEARTY

The aorta is the largest artery in the human body. Commonly seen clues are variations of "Blood line," "It comes from the heart," and "Major artery."

<<< **APART** >>>

THE ADVERB

Commonly seen clues: "Independently," "In pieces," "Isolated," "Not together," and "Separated."

<<< **APE** >>>

LITERALLY SPEAKING

Apes are nonhuman primates without tails, which distinguishes them from monkeys. The adjective "simian" can refer to either monkeys or apes. Apes seen in crossword clues include the chimpanzee, gibbon, gorilla, and orangutan, and filmdom's King Kong.

FIGURATIVELY SPEAKING

As a clumsy person, commonly seen clues include: "Big lug," "Bruiser," "Galoot," and "Lummox."

THE VERB

As a synonym for "mimic," commonly seen clues include "Copy," "Emulate," "Imitate," and "Parrot."

<<< **APER** >>>

THE IMITATOR

Commonly seen clues: "Copycat," "Impressionist," "Mimic," and "Unoriginal one."

<<< **APO** >>>

MILITARILY SPEAKING

Short for Army (or Air Force) Post Office, this abbreviation is used for mail going to U.S. military personnel overseas. Commonly seen clues are variations of "GI's mail drop" and "Mil. address."

<<< **APSE** >>>

IN CHURCH

Although the dictionary tells us that an apse is a recessed area in any building, it is virtually always clued as a section of a church, where it's near the nave.

<<< **APT** >>>

THE ADJECTIVE

As a synonym for "prone," commonly seen clues include "Disposed," "Inclined," and "Likely." Meaning "appropriate": "Fitting," "Suitable," and "Well-put." Meaning "intelligent": "Quick to learn" and "Very smart."

THE ABBREVIATION

As a short form of "apartment," commonly seen clues include "Envelope abbr.," "It may have an EIK" (short for "eat-in kitchen"), and "Rental dwelling: Abbr."

<<< **ARA** >>>

ON THE FIELD

Ara Parseghian was Notre Dame's football coach from 1964 to 1974.

IN THE SKY

The southern constellation Ara (Latin for "altar") is located near Scorpius.

─────── <<< **ARAB** >>> ───────

THE PERSON

Arabs are the majority in the Mideast nations of Abu Dhabi, Bahrain, Egypt, Iraq, Jordan, Kuwait, Oman, Qatar, Saudi Arabia, and Yemen. Arab men's traditional garb includes a burnoose (cloak) and kaffiyeh (headdress). The Arab (or Arabian) breed of horse is known for its intelligence, grace, and speed.

─────── <<< **ARAL** >>> ───────

ON THE MAP

The Asian inland Aral Sea is located between Kazakhstan and Uzbekistan. It has seen substantial shrinkage in recent years.

─────── <<< **ARAT** >>> ───────

COLLOQUIALLY SPEAKING

To "smell a rat" is to be suspicious of something. The phrase was used by Shakespeare in his play *Hamlet*.

Not So Fast!

"Clean thoroughly": S C _ U _

The answer can be SCOUR as well as the nearly synonymous SCRUB.

———— <<< **ARC** >>> ————

THE LINE

Commonly seen clues: "Circle section," "Curved line," "Eyebrow shape," "Fly-ball trajectory," and "Orbital path." The "line" of an arc can also be a figurative one, as in a temporary story line of a TV soap opera.

———— <<< **ARCH** >>> ————

THE NOUN

An arch may be a curved architectural feature, such as the famous ones in Paris and St. Louis, or a part of the foot or a shoe.

THE ADJECTIVE

As a synonym for "sly," commonly seen clues include: "Crafty," "Cunning," and "Roguish."

———— <<< **ARE** >>> ————

THE VERB

Commonly seen clues: "Exist," "Have being," and "Live and breathe."

IN TITLES

There's "All the Things You Are" (Jerome Kern tune), "Chances Are" (Johnny Mathis tune), *Diamonds Are Forever* (James Bond film), and "Where the Boys Are" (Connie Francis tune).

COLLOQUIALLY SPEAKING

Often-seen phrases include "Are we there yet?," "Are you serious?," "Who do you think you are?," and "You are here."

---⧐⧐ **AREA** ⧑⧑⧑---

GENERIC

Commonly seen clues include "Neck of the woods," "Neighborhood," "Region," "Sector," and "Vicinity." The word can also mean one's field of expertise or specialty.

MATHEMATICALLY SPEAKING

As it relates to a two-dimensional measure: "Carpet calculation," "Geographical stat," "Geometry finding," and "Square footage."

---⧐⧐ **ARENA** ⧑⧑⧑---

THE NOUN

Commonly seen clues: "Battleground," "Field of conflict," "Sports stadium," and "Where the action is."

---⧐⧐ **ARES** ⧑⧑⧑---

THE GOD

The Greek god Ares was the god of war, equivalent to the Romans' Mars. The son of Zeus and Hera, his children include the Amazons and Romulus and Remus.

---⧐⧐ **ARI** ⧑⧑⧑---

PEOPLE

Ari was the nickname of Greek shipping magnate Aristotle Onassis, second husband of Jacqueline Kennedy. Ari Fleischer is a former presidential press secretary. Actress Ari Meyers appeared on the sitcom *Kate & Allie*. Ari Ben Canaan is the main character in the Leon Uris novel *Exodus*, portrayed by Paul Newman in the film adaptation of the same name.

IN SPORTS

"ARI" is the abbreviation for the Arizona Diamondbacks major-league baseball team, as it often appears on scoreboards.

──── <<< **ARIA** >>> ────

IN MUSIC

An aria is a voice solo in an opera or oratorio. Clues will usually refer to well-known operas (such as *Carmen, Otello, Rigoletto,* and *Tosca*), opera singers (such as Kiri Te Kanawa, Luciano Pavarotti, Leontyne Price, and Beverly Sills), opera houses (such as the Met and La Scala), opera composers (such as Puccini and Verdi) or the arias themselves (such as *"Caro nome,"* "Summertime," and *"Vesti la giubba"*).

──── <<< **ARID** >>> ────

LITERALLY SPEAKING

As a synonym for "dry" as in "parched," commonly seen clues include "Desertlike," "Lacking water," "Like the Gobi," and "Saharan."

FIGURATIVELY SPEAKING

As a synonym for "dry" as in "uninteresting," commonly seen clues include "Jejune," "Uninspired," and "Vapid."

──── <<< **ARIEL** >>> ────

REAL PEOPLE

Ariel Sharon was prime minister of Israel from 2001 to 2006. Historian Ariel Durant collaborated with her husband Will on *The Story of Civilization.*

UNREAL PEOPLE, ETC.

Ariel is the title character of the Disney film *The Little Mermaid* and the sprite in Shakespeare's *The Tempest*. Ariel is also one of the moons of the planet Uranus.

———— <<< **ARISE** >>> ————

AS PEOPLE DO

Commonly seen clues: "Get out of bed," "Greet the day," and "Stand up."

AS THINGS DO

Ideas and events may arise also. Commonly seen clues in this sense: "Become evident," "Come to mind," "Crop up," and "Originate."

The past tense, "arose," actually appears in crosswords somewhat more often than "arise."

———— <<< **ARK** >>> ————

BIBLICALLY, ETC.

Human passengers on Noah's Ark included Noah and his wife, his three sons Ham, Shem, and Japheth and their wives; the Ark landed on Mount Ararat. Indiana Jones finds the Ark of the Covenant in *Raiders of the Lost Ark*. An ark is built by Steve Carell's character under the direction of the Supreme Being in the 2007 film *Evan Almighty*.

ON THE MAP

As an abbreviation for Arkansas, clues will most often refer either to the state's neighbors (Louisiana, Texas, Tennessee, Oklahoma, Missouri, Mississippi), its cities (Little Rock, Pine Bluff), or as the birthplace of President Bill Clinton.

———— ‹‹‹ **ARLES** ›››———

ON THE MAP

The French city of Arles, in the Provence region, is on the Rhône River. Vincent van Gogh painted some of his most famous works there.

———— ‹‹‹ **ARLO** ›››————

IN MUSIC

Folk singer Arlo Guthrie, son of balladeer Woody Guthrie, is best known for his 1960s' song "Alice's Restaurant."

IN THE PAPER

Arlo and Janis is a comic strip about a baby-boomer couple.

———— ‹‹‹ **ARM** ›››————

ON THE BODY

Commonly seen clues in this sense may reference arm bones (such as the ulna, humerus, and radius), arm muscles and joints (such as the biceps and elbow), or be more evocative (such as "Escort's offering," "Part of a shirt," "Pitcher's pride," and "Tattoo site").

ELSEWHERE

Other things with arms to keep in mind: chairs, phonographs, slot machines, sofas, and starfish.

THE VERB

Commonly seen clues in this sense include "Give guns to," "Prepare for battle," and "Provide with weapons."

<<< **ARNE** >>>

IN MUSIC

English composer Thomas Arne is best known for writing the anthem "Rule, Britannia!"

<<< **ARNO** >>>

ON THE MAP

Arno is an Italian river, flowing through the cities of Pisa and Florence.

THE ARTIST

The cartoons of Peter Arno appeared in *The New Yorker* from the 1920s to the 1960s.

<<< **ARR** >>>

THE ABBREVIATION

As a short form of "arrival," commonly seen clues are variations of "Airport stat.," "Flight board abbr.," "Opposite of dep." ("departure"), "Part of ETA" ("estimated time of arrival"), and "LAX posting." As a short form of "arrangement," commonly seen clues include "Band music abbr." and "Sheet music abbr."

<<< **ARS** >>>

LATIN FOR "ART"

Ars gratia artis ("Art for art's sake") is the motto of MGM. The expression *"Ars longa, vita brevis"* means "art endures, life is short." *Ars Poetica* ("The Art of Poetry") is a work by the Roman poet Horace. *Ars Amatoria* ("The Art of Love") is a long poem by the Roman poet Ovid.

THE LETTERS

As the plural of the spelled-out form of "R," commonly seen clues include "Ess preceders" and "Followers of cues" (the spelled-out form of "Qs").

———————— <<< **ART** >>> ————————

THE NOUN

Commonly seen clues in this sense include "Creative skill," "Critic's specialty," "Gallery display," "Illustrations," and "Painting or sculpture."

THE VERB

In this sense, it's the old-style form of "are." Juliet says "Wherefore art thou, Romeo" in Shakespeare's *Romeo and Juliet*, and the word is used in the Lord's Prayer.

THE PEOPLE

Celebrities named Art include columnist Buchwald, actor Carney, TV hosts Fleming and Linkletter, and jazz musicians Blakey and Tatum.

———————— <<< **ARTE** >>> ————————

FOREIGN FOR "ART"

As the Spanish word for "art," you'll see "Prado display" and "Goya works" (the Prado is a Madrid art museum; Goya was a

Spanish artist). As the Italian word for "art," you'll see the similar "Uffizi collection" and "Modigliani works" (the Uffizi Gallery is a Florence art museum; Modigliani was an Italian artist).

BLANKETY-BLANKS
Commedia dell'arte is a form of Italian theater. *"Vissi d'arte"* is an aria from the Puccini opera *Tosca*.

THE FUNNYMAN
Comedian Arte Johnson was a regular on the TV series *Laugh-In*.

<<< **ARTS** >>>

PARTNERSHIPS
"Crafts' partner," "Letters' partner," and "Sciences' partner" clue the phrases "arts and crafts," "arts and letters," and "arts and sciences."

PARTS
NEA is the National Endowment for the Arts, thus "NEA part" is a common clue for "ARTS." Similarly, there's the A&E (Arts and Entertainment) cable network, and the BA and MA college degrees.

FOLLOWERS
"Arts" can follow "graphic," "language," "lively," and "liberal" in common phrases.

<<< **ASA** >>>

SIMILES
"Cool __ cucumber," "Fit __ fiddle," "Flat __ pancake," "Hard

__ rock," "High __ kite," and "Smart __ whip" all clue AS A. "Simile center" hints at these without a fill-in-the-blank.

TO START WITH

Common phrases that start with "as a" are "as a matter of fact" and "as a rule."

THE PEOPLE

Asa Hutchinson is a former Arkansas congressman, Asa Gray was an American botanist, and Asa was the original first name of entertainer Al Jolson.

<<< ASAP >>>

THE ACRONYM

Short for "as soon as possible," commonly seen clues include: "Letters of urgency," "Memo directive," "PDQ," and "Pronto, in the office."

<<< ASCOT >>>

THE WEARABLE

An ascot is a broad necktie or scarf.

ON THE MAP

Ascot is the British site of a well-known racetrack, the setting of a scene in the musical *My Fair Lady*.

<<< ASEA >>>

ONE WORD

In the sense of "On the ocean," commonly seen clues are vari-

Not So Fast!

"Quarrel": S P A _

The answer can be SPAT or SPAR.

ants of "Between ports," "On the briny," "Sailing," and "Taking a cruise."

TWO WORDS

"Or to take arms against a sea of troubles" is part of the title character's famous "To be or not to be" soliloquy in Shakespeare's *Hamlet*.

<<< ASH >>>

THE TREE

Ash is a hardwood, used in the manufacture of baseball bats and hockey sticks.

THE RESIDUE

In this sense, ash is the powdery remains of burning, such as from volcanoes or fireplaces. Ash Wednesday is the first day of Lent.

THE COLORS

Ash can be a grayish blond or a silvery gray color.

─────── <<< **ASHE** >>> ───────

THE COURT GREAT

Tennis great Arthur Ashe, contemporary of Jimmy Connors and Bjorn Borg, won the men's Wimbledon title in 1975. The New York tennis stadium that is the site of the annual U.S. Open is named for him. Ashe's books include *Off the Court*, *A Hard Road to Glory*, and *Days of Grace*.

─────── <<< **ASHEN** >>> ───────

THE ADJECTIVE

As a synonym for "pale," commonly seen clues include: "Blanched," "Doughy," "Pallid," and "Wan."

─────── <<< **ASI** >>> ───────

BLANKETY-BLANKS

"__ was saying . . .", "__ live and breathe!" and "__ recall . . ." can all clue AS I. *As I Lay Dying* is a novel by William Faulkner, and "A Fool Such as I" is an Elvis Presley tune.

─────── <<< **ASIA** >>> ───────

ON THE MAP

The world's largest and most populous continent, ASIA is often clued by a country within it, such as China, India, Japan, Korea, Laos, and Thailand. The Himalayas, Siberia, and the Gobi Desert are all in Asia. The Ural Mountains mark part of the border between Europe and Asia.

─────── <<< **ASIDE** >>> ───────

THE NOUN

An aside is a "stage whisper," or a comment made by a stage

performer not intended for others in the cast, to be heard only by the audience. Off the stage, an aside can be any short digression.

THE ADVERB

Commonly seen clues in this sense: "In reserve," "Notwithstanding," "Out of the way," and "All kidding __."

<<< **ASIN** >>>

BLANKETY-BLANKS

"A __ 'apple'" to "Z __ 'zebra,'" and all the letters of the alphabet in between, are seen as clues for AS IN. "It's __ to Tell a Lie" (1930s popular song) clues A SIN.

<<< **ASIS** >>>

THE CAVEAT

As a warning to potential buyers, commonly seen clues include: "Auction proviso," "Not guaranteed," "Sales condition," "Warts and all," and "Without a warranty."

<<< **ASK** >>>

THE VERB

Commonly seen clues include: "Inquire," "Invite," "One way to learn," "Pop the question," "Query," and "Show curiosity."

<<< **ASP** >>>

MAN AND BEAST

The venomous snake that was the undoing of Cleopatra, it is also known as the Egyptian cobra and the horned viper. The Asp is a henchman of Daddy Warbucks in the *Little Orphan Annie* comic strip.

---- <<< **ASS** >>> ----

THE BEAST

Commonly seen clues include: "Beast of burden," "Brayer," "Pack animal," and "Wild equine."

THE PERSON

In this sense, commonly seen clues include: "Buffoon," "Bozo," "Dolt," "Knucklehead," "Ninny," "Obstinate cuss," and "Pompous sort."

---- <<< **ASSET** >>> ----

LITERALLY SPEAKING

In the accounting sense, commonly seen clues include: "Balance-sheet listing," "Item of value," "Liability's opposite," and "Stock or bond."

FIGURATIVELY SPEAKING

Less tangible assets include intelligence, poise, wisdom, and diplomacy, for example.

---- <<< **ASSN** >>> ----

THE ABBREVIATION

As a short form of "association," it is part of the names of the AARP, ABA, AMA, NAACP, NBA, NEA, PGA, PTA, and YMCA. Clued more synonymously, there's "Professional org.," "Special-interest grp.," and "Trade org."

⟪⟨⟨ ASST ⟩⟩⟩

THE ABBREVIATION

As a short form of "assistant," commonly seen clues include: "Aide: Abbr.," "CEO's helper," "Deputy: Abbr.," "Prof.'s rank," and "Type of D.A."

⟪⟨⟨ ASTA ⟩⟩⟩

THE DOG

Asta is the pet of detectives Nick and Nora Charles in the Dashiell Hammett novel *The Thin Man* and its film adaptations.

⟪⟨⟨ ASTI ⟩⟩⟩

ON THE MAP

The Italian province of Asti, in the Piedmont region, is famous for its wines. In particular, the sparkling wine known as Asti spumante originated there.

⟪⟨⟨ ASTO ⟩⟩⟩

IN LEGALESE

"As to" appears at the beginning of legal memos, where it is synonymous with "about," "concerning," "in the matter of," "in re," and "regarding."

⟪⟨⟨ ASTOR ⟩⟩⟩

THE SURNAME

Fur trader John Jacob Astor is believed to be the first American multimillionaire. Actress Mary Astor costarred with Humphrey Bogart in *The Maltese Falcon*.

ASTRO

IN SPORTS

Houston's major-league baseball team is the Astros.

IN TOONDOM

Astro is the dog of the title family in the futuristic animated sit-com *The Jetsons*.

ON THE ROAD

The Chevrolet Astro is a model of minivan produced from 1985 to 2005.

ATA

BLANKETY-BLANKS

"One __ time," "__ glance," "__ loss for words," "__ snail's pace," and "__ standstill" all clue AT A.

ATARI

THE COMPANY

Atari introduced the first commercially successful video game, Pong, in 1972.

ATE

See EAT.

ATEASE

IN THE ARMY

Commonly seen clues in this sense include "Drill order," "Military command," and "Relax, soldier."

OUT OF THE ARMY

Nonmilitary clues include "Hanging loose," "Lounging," and "Not worried."

<<< **ATEE** >>>

COLLOQUIALLY SPEAKING

To "suit to a tee" is to be perfect for a particular situation.

<<< **ATEST** >>>

THE BLAST

A-tests, short for "atomic tests," were tests of atomic weapons conducted by the U.S. in the 1940s and 1950s, in isolated locations such as Alamogordo, New Mexico, and Bikini and Eniwetok atolls in the South Pacific.

BLANKETY-BLANKS

"This is a test" or "This is only a test" is heard on the radio as stations test their emergency broadcast systems.

<<< **ATIT** >>>

COLLOQUIALLY SPEAKING

In the sense of "fighting," commonly seen clues include: "Arguing," "Bickering," and "Squabbling." In the sense of "busy": "Buckling down," "Hard at work," and "Plugging away."

BLANKETY-BLANKS

To "Have at it" is to fight, to "take a crack at it" is to try, and to "keep at it" is to persist.

─────────<<< **ATLAS** >>>─────────

THE LIFTER

Atlas, brother of Prometheus, was the mythical Titan who was condemned to support the sky on his shoulders.

THE BOOK

The book of maps gets its name from the mythical Atlas.

THE MISSILE

Atlas was the first U.S. intercontinental ballistic missile.

─────────<<< **ATNO** >>>─────────

IN CHEMISTRY

When clued as an abbreviation for "atomic number" (the number of protons in an atom's nucleus of an element), you'll see a number and an element, or the symbol for an element, such as "Copper's is 29: Abbr." or "26 for Fe, e.g."

BLANKETY-BLANKS

"At no time" means "never," and "at no cost" means "free."

Not So Fast!

"Open-eyed": A W A _ E

The answer can be AWAKE or AWARE.

<<< **ATO** >>>

BLANKETY-BLANK

"From __ Z (completely)" is the clue for A TO almost all of the time.

<<< **ATOM** >>>

IN SCIENCE

As it relates to chemistry or physics, commonly seen clues include "Building block of matter," "Energy source," "Fission subject," and "Molecule part."

THINKING SMALL

In the sense of something very small: "Little bit," "Scintilla," and "Tiny quantity."

<<< **ATONE** >>>

THE VERB

Commonly seen clues: "Expiate," "Do penance," "Make amends," and "Observe Yom Kippur" (the Jewish annual day of atonement).

<<< **ATOP** >>>

THE PREPOSITION

Commonly seen clues: "At the summit," "On the crest of," "Perched on," and "Surmounting."

<<< **ATRIA** >>>

PLACES IN THE HEART

Atria are heart chambers that receive blood from veins.

THE WIDE OPEN SPACES

Atria are also the central skylit lobbies that are often a part of modern office buildings and hotels.

———— ‹‹‹ **ATSEA** ›››› ————

COLLOQUIALLY SPEAKING

Although dictionaries tell us that both "asea" and "at sea" can mean "confused," "asea" is never clued this way in puzzles, while "at sea" is clued in this sense most of the time, such as "Baffled," "Befuddled," "Clueless," and "Perplexed."

LITERALLY SPEAKING

Commonly seen clues in this sense are similar to those for "asea," such as "Between ports," "On the briny," "Sailing," and "Taking a cruise."

———— ‹‹‹ **ATT** ›››› ————

LEGALLY SPEAKING

As a short form of "attorney," commonly seen clues include: "ABA member" (American Bar Association), "Courtroom fig.," and "Lawyer: Abbr."

MA BELL

Though the large telephone company is properly known as AT&T, you'll sometimes see telephonic clues for ATT like "Long-distance letters."

——— <<< **ATTA** >>> ———

ENCOURAGING WORDS

"__ boy!" and "__ girl!" are the two clues that appear most often.

THE MIDDLE NAME

Atta is the middle name of former U.N. secretary-general Kofi Annan.

——— <<< **AUNT** >>> ———

GENERIC

Nonspecific clues are variations of "First cousin's mother," "Family member," "Mom's sister," and "Reunion attendee."

ACTUAL

Real-life aunts you may see include Jane Fonda (to Bridget), Princess Anne (to Princes William and Harry), and singer Rosemary Clooney (to George).

FICTIONAL

There's Opie's Aunt Bee (*Andy Griffith Show*), Dorothy's Aunt Em (*The Wizard of Oz*), Tom Sawyer's Aunt Polly, and the pancake-box portrait of Aunt Jemima.

——— <<< **AURA** >>> ———

THE ATMOSPHERE

Commonly seen clues: "Ambiance," "Distinctive air," "New Age glow," and "Subtle quality."

Need to Know: Crossword German 101

The 10 German words that appear most often as crossword answers (diacritical marks, if any, are omitted):

ach (oh)	*herr* (mister)
das (the)	*ich* (I)
drei (three)	*ost* (east)
eine (a)	*sie* (you)
eins (one)	*uber* (above)

<<< **AVA** >>>

THE ACTRESS

Ava Gardner was married at one time to singer Frank Sinatra, bandleader Artie Shaw, and actor Mickey Rooney.

<<< **AVE** >>>

THE ABBREVIATION

As a short form of "avenue," generic clues include "City map abbr.," "St. crosser," and "Urban rd." Specific avenues often seen are New York City's Madison and Lexington, and Washington, D.C.'s Pennsylvania and Constitution.

IN LATIN

As an old Roman word of greeting meaning "hail," clues are variations of "Forum welcome" and "Greeting to Galba." "Ave Maria" is a Roman Catholic prayer.

⟪⟪⟪ AVER ⟫⟫⟫

THE VERB

Commonly seen clues: "Assert," "Declare," "Maintain," "Profess," and "State confidently."

INSIDER'S TIP: "Aver" and "avow" are nearly synonymous, and the same clues are often seen for both words. That's why experienced puzzlers always wait for crossing-clue verification before filling in the last two letters of "A V _ _."

⟪⟪⟪ AVIS ⟫⟫⟫

THE COMPANY

Avis Rent-a-Car, founded in 1946, has been using the slogan "We Try Harder" since the 1960s. Its competitors include Alamo, Budget, Dollar, Enterprise, Hertz, and National.

IN LATIN

"*Avis*" is the Latin word for "bird." The Latin idiom "*rara avis*" means "rare bird," or anything out of the ordinary.

⟪⟪⟪ AVON ⟫⟫⟫

THE RIVER

Avon is the name of at least four different rivers in Great Britain, but in crosswords it's always the one that flows through the town of Stratford-Upon-Avon, home of William Shakespeare, a.k.a. "the Bard."

THE COMPANY

Avon Products is primarily in the perfume and cosmetics business, its memorable "Avon calling" TV commercials featuring a salesperson ringing a homeowner's doorbell. Its competitors include Revlon and Mary Kay.

───── ‹‹‹ **AVOW** ›››─────

THE VERB

Commonly seen clues: "Admit openly," "Assert," "Declare," "Maintain," and "Swear."

(See also AVER.)

───── ‹‹‹ **AWAIT** ›››─────

THE VERB

Commonly seen clues: "Anticipate," "Be patient for," "Lie ahead," and "Look forward to."

───── ‹‹‹ **AWARE** ›››─────

THE ADJECTIVE

Commonly seen clues: "Clued in," "Cognizant," "Conscious," "In the know," "Mindful," and "With it."

Not So Fast!

"Norse explorer": E R I _

There are two acceptable ways to spell his name: ERIC and ERIK.

⟨⟨⟨ AWE ⟩⟩⟩

THE NOUN

Commonly seen noun clues: "Amazement," "Reverence," "Veneration," and "Wonderment."

THE VERB

As a verb, there's: "Blow away," "Bowl over," "Flabbergast," "Impress greatly," and "Wow."

⟨⟨⟨ AWOL ⟩⟩⟩

THE ACRONYM

The military term AWOL is short for "absent without leave," and may be used as an adjective, adverb (as in "go AWOL"), or noun (for the soldier guilty of the offense). Commonly seen clues: "Army no-show," "GI's offense," "Mil. truant," and "MP's quarry."

⟨⟨⟨ AXE ⟩⟩⟩

THE TOOL

People using axes include firefighters, loggers, lumberjacks (the legendary Paul Bunyan, specifically), and the Tin Woodman from *The Wizard of Oz*. Tomahawks and hatchets are two kinds of axes. As a verb meaning "to wield an ax," clues are variations of "Chop down."

THE JOB VERB

As a synonym for "dismiss from a job," commonly seen clues include: "Can," "Fire," "Let go," and "Pink-slip."

---<<< **AXLE** >>>---

ON A VEHICLE

An axle is the bar that connects two wheels of an automobile, covered wagon, etc. Vehicle charges on toll roads are often based on the number of axles that the vehicle has.

ERNESTO "CHE" GUEVARA, 1960.
(MUSEO CHE GUEVARA, HAVANA)

the

LETTERS
B–C

───<<< **BAA** >>>───

IN THE FIELD

As the bleat or sound made by a sheep, commonly seen clues include: "Cote call," "Lamb's cry," "Ram's remark," and the immortal "Ewe said it."

───<<< **BAR** >>>───

THE VERB

As a synonym for "prevent," commonly seen clues include "Block," "Eliminate," "Keep out," and "Prohibit."

EATING AND DRINKING PLACES

As a place to drink, commonly seen clues include "Grill partner," "Pub," and "Tavern." There are also salad bars, sushi bars, and piano bars.

THE SHAPE

Bar-shaped things include candy and chocolate, soap, certain graphs, slot-machine symbols, and gold ingots.

IN LAW

"The bar" is a symbol for the legal profession.

───<<< **BAS** >>>───

THE DEGREES

"BAs" is short for Bachelor of Science college degrees.

IN ART

A bas-relief is a type of sculpture.

<<< **BASE** >>>

ON THE DIAMOND

The bases in baseball include first, second, third, and home plate. Infielders are stationed at each of the first three.

IN CHEMISTRY

A base (a.k.a. "alkali") is a chemical compound that can neutralize an acid.

OTHER NOUNS

A base can be a military installation, a headquarters, or a foundation.

THE ADJECTIVE

In this sense, commonly seen clues include "Despicable," "Lowly," "Mean," and "Not refined."

<<< **BAT** >>>

IN SPORTS

Bats are used in cricket as well as baseball. The best-known brand of baseball bat is the Louisville Slugger.

THE BEAST

Bats are flying mammals that live in caves. Vampires, Count Dracula in particular, can take the form of a bat.

<<< **BEA** >>>

THE ACTRESS

Bea Arthur starred in the sitcoms *Maude* and *The Golden Girls*.

BLANKETY-BLANKS

The songs "Luck Be a Lady" and "Be a Clown," and the game show *Who Wants to Be a Millionaire* may be used to clue BE A.

———— <<< **BEE** >>> ————

THE GATHERINGS

There are spelling bees, quilting bees, and husking bees.

THE INSECT

"Apiary resident," "Buzzer," "Honey handler," "Nectar collector," and "Stinger" all clue the insect directly. Jerry Seinfeld provided the voice of bee Barry B. Benson in the 2007 animated film *Bee Movie*.

IN THE NEWS

Sacramento and Fresno both have daily newspapers known as the *Bee*.

———— <<< **BEN** >>> ————

THE CELEBRITIES

Entertainers named Ben include Affleck, Gazzara, Kingsley, Stiller, and Vereen. Two golf Bens are Crenshaw and Hogan. There's also Federal Reserve head Bernanke, author Hecht, artist Shahn, and Ben & Jerry's ice cream.

———— <<< **BOA** >>> ————

THE SNAKE

Commonly seen clues in this sense: "Amazon squeezer," "__ constrictor," and "Snake with a squeeze."

WHAT TO WEAR

A boa can also be a scarf or stole made of feathers, fur, or fabric.

————— <<< **BRA** >>> —————

WHAT TO WEAR

Commonly seen clues in this sense: "Bikini part," "Lingerie item," and "Victoria's Secret buy." Other well-known bra manufacturers include Bali, Olga, and Maidenform.

ON A CAR

A bra may also be a removable cover for an automobile that protects the grille from road debris.

————— <<< **BRIE** >>> —————

THE CHEESE

Brie is a soft cheese named for the French province where it originated. It is similar to Camembert, another soft French cheese.

————— <<< **BUS** >>> —————

THE RIDE

Commonly seen clues for the vehicle include "Greyhound, for example," "Motor coach," "Public transportation," and "School vehicle." In the sitcom *The Honeymooners*, Jackie Gleason portrays bus driver Ralph Kramden. The 1994 action film *Speed* takes place on a city bus.

THE VERB

To "bus" is to assist a waiter in clearing a dining table of dishes.

Not So Fast!

"Fissure": R _ _ T

The answer can be RIFT or RENT.

‹‹‹ CAAN ›››

FATHER AND SON

Actor James Caan portrayed Sonny Corleone in *The Godfather*. His other starring roles include the films *Misery* and *Honeymoon in Vegas* and the TV series *Las Vegas*. His son Scott is also an actor.

‹‹‹ CANE ›››

THE WALKING STICK

A cane is associated with Old West lawman Bat Masterson, comedian Charlie Chaplin, and Planters mascot Mr. Peanut. Candy in the shape of a cane is popular in the Christmas season.

BOTANICALLY SPEAKING

Sugar is obtained from one type of cane. Bamboo and rattan are two other types.

‹‹‹ CANOE ›››

ON THE WATER

Commonly seen clues: "Birch-bark creation," "Dugout," "Hiawatha's transport," "Kayak kin," "Lake boat," and "Paddled craft."

<<< **CAP** >>>

WHAT TO WEAR

As an item of headgear, types of caps include the beret, tam-o'-shanter, and beanie. Baseball players, golfers, and graduating students wear caps, as do toothpaste tubes and ballpoint pens.

YOU'RE THE TOP

"Cap" can also mean "limit," as either a noun (such as "Salary maximum") or a verb ("Put a lid on").

<<< **CAR** >>>

ON THE ROAD

Any make or model of automobile is fair game as a clue. They can be tricky to figure out when they're also the names of other things, like Mercury, Saturn, and Jaguar.

OFF THE ROAD

Elevators, trains, and roller coasters also have cars.

<<< **CARE** >>>

THE VERB

Commonly seen clues: "Be concerned," "Give a hoot," and "Worry."

THE NOUN

Variations of "Attention to detail," "Diligence," "Mindfulness," and "Supervision" clue CARE as a noun, as does "Part of TLC" (tender loving care).

———— <<< **CAT** >>> ————

TYPES

Breeds of house cats often seen include the Abyssinian, Burmese, Persian, and Siamese. Other house-cat categories are the calico and tabby. Any type of wild feline, such as the leopard or tiger, may also clue CAT.

FELINE CELEBRITIES

In cartoons, there's Felix, Garfield, Heathcliff, and Stimpy, and there's Morris in TV commercials. The title characters in the Andrew Lloyd Webber musical *Cats* include Grizabella, Macavity, and Rum Tum Tugger.

THE PERSON

A "cat" may also be a "cool" person, particularly a lover of jazz music.

———— <<< **CENT** >>> ————

MONEY WORLDWIDE

In addition to the U.S., countries with cent coins include Canada, Australia, and all the European countries that use the euro (such as France, Italy, and Spain).

———— <<< **CHE** >>> ————

THE PEOPLE

Revolutionary Ernesto "Che" Guevara was an associate of Fidel Castro. A character named Che is the narrator of the Andrew Lloyd Webber musical *Evita*, portrayed by Antonio Banderas in the film version.

--- <<< **CIA** >>> ---

THE SPIES

Based in Langley, Virginia, and nicknamed "The Company," the Central Intelligence Agency handles foreign intelligence gathering. Its recent directors have included George H. W. Bush, Michael Hayden, Robert Gates, Porter Goss, and George Tenet. Its World War II–era predecessor was the OSS (Office of Strategic Services). Its Cold War–era Soviet counterpart was the KGB.

--- <<< **CITE** >>> ---

THE VERB

Commonly seen clues: "Allude to," "Give a traffic ticket to," "Give as an example," "Mention," and "Quote."

--- <<< **COLA** >>> ---

THE CARBONATED SOFT DRINK

Colas are served at fast-food restaurants and vending machines. The most popular brands are Coke, Pepsi, RC, and Jolt. Cola is an ingredient in the rum cocktail known as the Cuba libre.

--- <<< **CREE** >>> ---

THE NATIVE AMERICANS

The Cree reside mostly in the Canadian provinces of Quebec, Manitoba, and Saskatchewan.

--- <<< **CSA** >>> ---

THE ABBREVIATION

Short for "Confederate States of America," commonly seen clues include "Civil War initials," "Jefferson Davis org.," and "1860s' insignia."

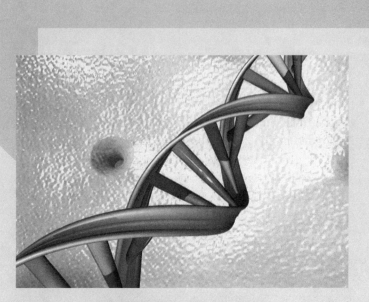

THE DOUBLE HELIX STRUCTURE OF DNA.
(NATIONAL HUMAN GENOME RESEARCH INSTITUTE)

the

LETTER

D

―――――― <<< **DAN** >>> ――――――

THE PEOPLE

There's actor Aykroyd, novelist Brown, football great Marino, former vice president Quayle, and TV newsman Rather.

OTHERS

A "dapper Dan" is a well-dressed fellow. In lowercase, a dan is a skill level in martial arts.

―――――― <<< **DAR** >>> ――――――

THE ORGANIZATION

The Daughters of the American Revolution is a patriotic group whose members can trace their ancestry to someone who helped achieve American independence.

ON THE MAP

Dar es Salaam is the largest city in Tanzania.

―――――― <<< **DARE** >>> ――――――

THE CHALLENGE

Commonly seen clues: "Act of defiance," "Be bold," "Have the nerve," "Take a risk," and "Venture."

―――――― <<< **DAS** >>> ――――――

THE ABBREVIATION

As a short form of "district attorneys," commonly seen clues include "Courtroom VIPs," "Prosecutors: Abbr.," and "Some govt. lawyers."

THE FOREIGN WORD

"Das" is one of the German words for "the," as it appears in the title of a Richard Wagner opera (*Das Rheingold*) and a Karl Marx book (*Das Kapital*).

‹‹‹ DDS ›››

THE ABBREVIATION

DDS stands for Doctor of Dental Surgery, a degree awarded to dentists. Most crossword clues for DDS avoid "dentist," because of the "Dental" in DDS. So you'll see such evasions as "Driller's deg." and "Tooth examiner's letters."

‹‹‹ DEE ›››

THE LETTER

As the spelled-out version of the letter D, you'll see academic references like "Barely passing" and "Poor grade."

THE LAST NAME

There are actresses Ruby and Sandra (Gidget portrayer in the movies), and singers Kiki and Joey.

FIRST AND MIDDLE NAMES

There's actress Dee Wallace and actor Billy Dee Williams.

Not So Fast!

"Thin opening": S L _ T

The answer can be SLOT or SLIT.

ON THE MAP

Scotland's River Dee flows through the city of Aberdeen and near Balmoral Castle.

———— <<< **DEER** >>> ————

THE BEAST

Commonly seen clues: "Antlered animal," "Moose relative," "Timid creature," "Venison source," and "Woodland beast."

INSIDER'S TIP: Keep in mind that the plural of "deer" is also "deer," so the plural form of all the previous clues are also correct for DEER.

———— <<< **DEL** >>> ————

ON THE MAP

As an abbreviation for Delaware (the first state to ratify the U.S. Constitution), you'll see references to its cities (such as Dover and Wilmington) and its neighboring states of Md., N.J., and Pa. Tierra del Fuego is a group of islands at the southern tip of South America. The Costa del Sol is a resort region of southern Spain.

THE PEOPLE

Actor Benicio del Toro won an Academy Award for his role in the 1998 film *Traffic*. Singer Del Shannon is best known for the 1961 tune "Runaway."

———— <<< **DELI** >>> ————

THE STORE

A deli, short for "delicatessen," is a neighborhood store where sandwiches, cold cuts, etc., are sold. By extension, it is also the department of a supermarket where these items are found.

<<< DEN >>>

FOR ANIMALS

A den is a lair for wild animals, such as lions and bears.

FOR PEOPLE

The den of a home (a.k.a. "study" or "family room") is usually thought of as a cozy place for relaxation. A den is also a group of Cub Scouts.

<<< DENT >>>

ON A CAR

Usually defined in this sense as a variation of "Body-shop repair" and "Fender damage."

FIGURATIVELY SPEAKING

One makes a dent in a project if there has been small but noticeable progress made toward completing it.

<<< DES >>>

ON THE MAP

"__ Moines, Iowa" and "__ Plaines, Ill." (a suburb of Chicago) are by far the two most popular clues for DES.

<<< DIANE >>>

THE PEOPLE

There are actresses Keaton, Ladd, and Lane, TV journalist Sawyer, and fashion designer von Furstenberg. Diane Chambers was Shelley Long's role on the sitcom *Cheers*. Presumably named after a person, Steak Diane is prepared with filet mignon.

⫷⫷ DISC ⫸⫸

THE RECORDINGS

"Disc" can be the "D" of CD (Compact Disc). Phonograph records are also called "discs."

THE SHAPE

Disc-shaped things often referred to in crossword clues include checkers, Frisbees, platters, and lozenges.

⫷⫷ DNA ⫸⫸

THAT'S LIFE

Common clues such as "Genetic material" and "Substance in cells" can define RNA as well as DNA. "Chromosome component," "Double-helix molecule," and "High-tech fingerprint" are unique to DNA.

⫷⫷ DOE ⫸⫸

THE ANIMAL

A doe is a female deer, rabbit, or kangaroo.

THE SURNAME

The names John Doe and Jane Doe are used for unidentified men and women in legal proceedings.

⫷⫷ DON ⫸⫸

THE GUYS

There are actors Adams and Cheadle, author DeLillo, singer Everly, Hawaiian entertainer Ho, actor Johnson, boxing promoter King, actor Knotts, TV announcer Pardo, and comedian Rickles. The term "don" can apply to the head of a crime syndicate.

THE VERB

Commonly seen clues in this sense: "Put on" and "Slip into."

<<< **DOOR** >>>

THE PORTAL

Commonly seen clues: "Entryway," "It may swing or revolve," "Way in," and "Way out."

<<< **DOS** >>>

HIGH-TECH

DOS (short for "disk operating system") preceded Windows as the "master program" used by most personal computers.

THE PLURAL

As the plural of "do," it can refer to hairdos, parties, or requirements (as in "do's and don'ts").

SOUTH OF THE BORDER

"*Dos*" is the Spanish word for "two."

THE WRITER

Author John Dos Passos wrote the fiction trilogy *U.S.A.*

<<< **DOT** >>>

LITERALLY SPEAKING

Commonly seen "direct" clues include "Period," "Point," "Speck," and "Tiny circle."

SYMBOLICALLY SPEAKING

A dot is the Morse code symbol for E, part of Braille writing, and part of a semicolon, ellipsis (the " . . . " in trailed-off sentences) and umlaut (the two-dot symbol on German words). "Dot com" is the ending for commercial Web-site addresses (a.k.a. URLs).

THE ABBREVIATION

DOT may stand for the U.S. Department of Transportation.

<<< DRAT >>>

THE MILD OATH

Commonly seen clues are variations of "Darn it!," "Fiddlesticks!," and "Phooey!." It was uttered by W. C. Fields more than once in his films.

<<< DRAW >>>

THE VERBS

Artists draw, as do poker players, tourist attractions, and Old West gunfighters.

THE NOUN

A contest without a clear winner (such as a chess match or wrestling bout) is a draw.

<<< DRED >>>

MR. SCOTT

The 1857 Dred Scott Decision of the U.S. Supreme Court was one of the contributing factors of the Civil War.

THE BOOK

Dred is an 1856 novel by Harriet Beecher Stowe, whose title character was derived from the Dred Scott case.

AN EMU. (FOTOLIA.COM)

the

LETTER

E

⫷⫷⫷ **EAR** ⫸⫸⫸

THE NOUN

In addition to the organ of hearing, it is a portion of corn on the cob, a handle of a jug or large pitcher, as well as musical discernment. The anvil, hammer, and stirrup are three small bones located inside the ear.

⫷⫷⫷ **EARL** ⫸⫸⫸

THE TITLE

Earl is a British title of nobility, below a marquis and above a viscount. The wife of an earl is a countess.

THE FIRST NAME

Bowler Anthony, jazz pianist Hines, actor Holliman, banjoist Scruggs, Supreme Court justice Warren, and baseball manager Weaver are well-known Earls.

THE MIDDLE NAME

Earl is the middle name of President Jimmy Carter and actor James Earl Jones.

⫷⫷⫷ **EARN** ⫸⫸⫸

THE VERB

Commonly seen clues: "Bring home," "Deserve," "Have coming," and "Merit."

⫷⫷⫷ **EASE** ⫸⫸⫸

THE VERB

Commonly seen verb clues include "Alleviate," "Facilitate," "Lighten," and "Simplify."

THE NOUN

As a synonym for "freedom from concern" or "freedom from difficulty," there's "Comfort," "Fluency," "Naturalness," and "Relaxation."

———— <<< **EAST** >>> ————

THE DIRECTION

"Compass point," "Right, on a map," "Sunrise direction," and "Toward the dawn" all commonly clue EAST. East is also one of the four players in the game of bridge.

ON THE MAP

"The East" may denote the eastern part of the U.S., or the Asian region a.k.a. "the Orient." "Down East" is a nickname for the state of Maine. The East River separates the island of Manhattan from the other New York City boroughs of Brooklyn and Queens.

IN SPORTS

The Big East is a college football conference, and the major professional sports leagues have East (or Eastern) divisions.

Not So Fast!

"Born first": _ L D E R

The answer can be OLDER or the nearly synonymous ELDER.

<<< **EASY** >>>

THE ADJECTIVE

Commonly seen clues: "Effortless," "Elementary," "Lenient," "Not difficult," and "Simple."

THE EXCLAMATION

"Calm down!," "No problem!," and "Piece of cake!" can clue EASY used as an interjection.

<<< **EAT** >>>

FOODWISE

Commonly seen clues are variations of "Consume," "Dig in!," "Have dinner," and "Mother's directive."

OTHER MEANINGS

EAT may also be a synonym for "erode" or "corrode," and is a slang term meaning "absorb, as a financial loss."

The past tense, "ate," actually appears a bit more often in crosswords than "eat."

<<< **EATS** >>>

SLANGILY SPEAKING

Separate from the meanings of EAT mentioned above, "eats" is a slang term for "food," which is supposedly seen on signs for informal eateries such as diners.

<<< **EAVE** >>>

ON THE HOUSE

An eave is an overhanging lower edge of a roof, where icicles may form in the winter.

———— <<< **EAU** >>> ————

LE NOUN

"*Eau*" is the French word for "water," which is its literal meaning in "Eau de Cologne" and "eau de vie" (a French brandy). Eau Claire is a city in Wisconsin.

———— <<< **EBAN** >>> ————

THE STATESMAN

South African–born Abba Eban was Israel's ambassador to the United Nations and the United States in the 1940s and 1950s, its deputy prime minister in the 1960s, and its foreign minister in the 1960s and 1970s. His books include *Voice of Israel* and *Diplomacy for a New Century*. He is a member of the very exclusive club of celebrities whose first and last names are crossword regulars (actor Alan Alda is another).

———— <<< **EBB** >>> ————

THE VERB

Commonly seen clues: "Diminish," "Flow's partner," "Recede," "Slacken," and "Withdraw."

THE MAN

Lyricist Fred Ebb collaborated with composer John Kander on the musicals *Cabaret*, *Chicago*, and *New York, New York*.

———— <<< **ECHO** >>> ————

THROUGH THE AIR

Commonly seen clues: "Canyon sound effect," "Resound," "Reverberate," and "Sonic bounce."

TO THE GREEKS

In Greek mythology, Echo was a nymph who had an unrequited love for Narcissus.

<<< **ECLAT** >>>

FROM THE FRENCH

As a synonym for "brilliant success," commonly seen clues include "Acclaim," "Dazzle," "Fanfare," and "Showy display."

<<< **ECO** >>>

THE MAN

The books of Italian author Umberto Eco include *Baudolino, Foucault's Pendulum,* and *The Name of the Rose.*

THE PREFIX

"Eco-friendly," "ecosystem," and "ecotourism" all start with the "green" prefix ECO-.

INSIDER'S TIP: Though it may seem as if it should be, "eco." is not an abbreviation for "economics." That would be "econ."

<<< **ECRU** >>>

THE COLOR

Ecru is a light brown, often the color of curtains, hosiery, linen, and silk.

<<< **EDAM** >>>

THE SPREADABLE

Edam is a mild yellow cheese named for the Dutch town where it is made. It is typically sold in spheres, coated with wax.

──────<<< EDDY >>>──────

THE WATER

Commonly seen clues: "Countercurrent," "Sea swirl," "Vortex," and "Whirlpool."

THE PEOPLE

Mary Baker Eddy founded the religion of Christian Science. Actor Nelson Eddy costarred with Jeanette MacDonald in a series of film musicals in the 1930s and 1940s. Duane Eddy is a Grammy-winning rock guitarist.

──────<<< EDEN >>>──────

THE PARADISE

In Genesis, Eden was the garden paradise where Adam and Eve lived. The word can also refer to any blissful or delightful place.

THE PEOPLE

Anthony Eden was a 1950s British prime minister, whose title was Earl of Avon. Actress Barbara Eden is best known for her title role in the sitcom *I Dream of Jeannie*.

──────<<< EDGE >>>──────

THE NOUN

In the literal sense, commonly seen clues include "Border," "Brink," "Fringe," "Margin," and "Rim." Meaning "competitive advantage," there's "Head start" and "Upper hand."

THE VERB

As a verb, it can mean to sharpen, or to defeat by a narrow margin.

⟨⟨⟨ EDIE ⟩⟩⟩

THE PEOPLE

Actress Edie Falco appeared in the TV series *The Sopranos*. Singer Edie Adams was married to comedian Ernie Kovacs. Less-often seen Edies include singer Brickell and the girlfriend of the title character in the TV series *Peter Gunn*.

⟨⟨⟨ EDIT ⟩⟩⟩

THE VERB

Commonly seen clues: "Blue-pencil," "Do newspaper work," "Improve prose," "Revise," and "Work on galleys." "Edit" is also a command in word-processing programs.

⟨⟨⟨ EDNA ⟩⟩⟩

REAL

There are authors Buchanan, Ferber, and O'Brien, and poet St. Vincent Millay.

FICTIONAL

Edna Krabappel is Bart's teacher in the animated sitcom *The Simpsons*. Dame Edna Everage is the alter ego of British comedian Barry Humphries. Edna, portrayed by John Travolta, is the mother of Tracy Turnblad in the 2007 film *Hairspray*.

⟨⟨⟨ EDS ⟩⟩⟩

THE PEOPLE

Men named Ed who are often paired to get EDS include former New York City mayor Koch, TV personalities Bradley, McMahon, and Sullivan, and actors Asner, Begley, and O'Neill.

THE ABBREVIATION

As a short form for "editors," commonly seen clues are variations of "Mag. workers," "Masthead figs.," and "Newspaper execs."

———————— <<< **EDSEL** >>> ————————

THE CAR

Edsel was an unsuccessful model of Ford automobile that was sold from 1958 to 1960. It was named for Edsel Ford, only son of company founder Henry Ford.

———————— <<< **EEE** >>> ————————

THE SHOE SPECIFICATION

EEE in a shoe or on a shoebox indicates a very wide shoe of a particular size.

Need to Know: Crossword Italian 101

The 10 Italian words that appear most often as crossword answers:

amore (love)	*essa* (they, also *esso*)
arte (art)	*mia* (my, also *mio*)
cara (dear, also *caro*)	*sera* (evening)
ciao (good-bye)	*tre* (three)
ella (she)	*vino* (wine)

<<< **EEK** >>>

THE EXCLAMATION

A cry of fright seen in comic strips, often at the sight of a mouse.

<<< **EEL** >>>

THE FISH

A snakelike fish, a.k.a. "conger" or "moray," some of which carry an electrical charge. Eels are proverbially slippery fish, hence the simile "slippery as an eel." A sniggler is a fisherman who catches eels. The Japanese word for eel is *unagi*, often seen in sushi bars where eels are served.

INSIDER'S TIP: The plural of "eel" can be either "eels" or "eel."

<<< **EEN** >>>

THE ADVERB

As a poetical term for "evening," EEN may be clued with "dusk," "nightfall," or "twilight."

THE SUFFIX

-EEN may be added to the words "velvet" and "hallow" to form new words.

<<< **EER** >>>

THE ADVERB

A poetical term for "ever" or "always."

THE SUFFIX

As an "occupational" suffix, EER can be added to words such as "auction," "chariot," "mountain," and "musket."

—————— <<< **EERIE** >>> ——————

THE ADJECTIVE

Commonly seen clues: "Creepy," "Like a haunted house," "Spooky," "Strange," "Uncanny," and "Weird."

—————— <<< **EERO** >>> ——————

THE ARCHITECT

Finnish architect Eero Saarinen designed St. Louis's Gateway Arch. His father Eliel was also an architect.

—————— <<< **EGAD** >>> ——————

THE OLD-TIME EXCLAMATION

Commonly seen clues: "Mild oath," "My goodness!," "Yikes!," and "Zounds!" Fictional characters Dr. Watson (Sherlock Holmes's pal) and Major Hoople (from the old comic strip) were known to utter it.

Not So Fast!

"Fizzy drink": _ O _ A

The answer can be SODA or COLA.

———— <<< **EGAN** >>> ————

THE PEOPLE

Edward Cardinal Egan became Archbishop of New York in 2000. Big Apple police officer Eddie Egan inspired the character portrayed by Gene Hackman in *The French Connection*. Actor Richard Egan appeared in such films as *A Summer Place* and *Love Me Tender*. William Egan was the first governor of the state of Alaska.

———— <<< **EGG** >>> ————

THE EDIBLE

Commonly seen clues: "Heckler's missile," "Omelet ingredient," "Poultry product," and the slang term "Cackleberry."

THE INEDIBLES

Silly Putty comes in a plastic egg. In the sitcom *Mork and Mindy*, Robin Williams's alien character comes to Earth in an egg-shaped spaceship. Fabergé eggs are highly prized collectibles.

THE VERB

To "egg on" is to prod or provoke.

———— <<< **EGO** >>> ————

IN PSYCHOLOGY

Derived from the Latin word for "I," the ego is the part of the psyche that experiences and reacts to the outside world. In common usage, "Conceit," "Self-esteem," and "Swelled head" all clue EGO.

<<< EINE >>>

IN GERMANY

"Eine" is the German word for the English article "a." *Eine kleine Nachtmusik* ("A little serenade") is a work by Mozart.

INSIDER'S TIP: Don't confuse EINE with the similar EINS, which is German for "one" (the number).

<<< EIRE >>>

ON THE MAP

EIRE is the Irish name for the island of Ireland (a.k.a. "Hibernia" and "The Emerald Isle") as well as for the Republic of Ireland, whose major cities include Dublin, Cork, Galway, and Limerick. "Eire" may be seen on euro coins that originate in the Republic of Ireland.

<<< EKE >>>

THE VERB

To "eke out" is to supplement, to barely get by, or to achieve with difficulty, as in "eke out a living."

<<< ELAL >>>

THE CARRIER

El Al is the national airline of Israel. Its hub is Ben Gurion Airport, outside of Tel Aviv.

<<< ELAN >>>

THE FEELING

As a synonym for "enthusiasm," commonly seen clues include "Gusto," "Joie de vivre," "Pizazz," "Verve," "Zest," and "Zing."

⟨⟨⟨ ELATE ⟩⟩⟩

THE VERB

Commonly seen clues: "Cheer up," "Delight," "Gladden," "Overjoy," and "Tickle pink."

⟨⟨⟨ ELBA ⟩⟩⟩

THE ISLAND

Located off the western coast of Italy near Corsica, Elba was the island where former French emperor Napoleon was exiled in 1814. Napoleon is the supposed speaker of the phrase "Able was I ere I saw Elba"—a palindrome because it reads the same from right to left or from left to right.

⟨⟨⟨ ELECT ⟩⟩⟩

THE VERB

Commonly seen clues: "Campaign button word," "Choose," "Put into office," and "Vote in."

⟨⟨⟨ ELEE ⟩⟩⟩

THE GENERAL

General Robert E. Lee commanded the eastern army of the Confederate States of America during the Civil War. "Waiting for the Robert E. Lee" is a popular song of the 1910s about a steamboat.

⟨⟨⟨ ELENA ⟩⟩⟩

THE NAME

Elena Dementieva is a Russian-born tennis pro. Spain's Princess Elena is the daughter of King Juan Carlos. Actress Elena

Verdugo appeared on the TV series *Marcus Welby, M.D.* "Maria Elena" is a 1940s tune popularized by Jimmy Dorsey and his orchestra.

⟨⟨⟨ ELI ⟩⟩⟩

THE NAME

There's pro quarterback Manning, actor Wallach, and cotton gin inventor Whitney. In the Old Testament, Eli is a Hebrew priest who trained the young prophet Samuel. The middle name of pioneer automaker Ransom Olds was Eli.

SCHOLASTICALLY SPEAKING

An Eli is any student of Yale University, coined for the school's benefactor, Elihu Yale. So any celebrity who attended Yale might be seen as a crossword clue similar to "Meryl Streep, once." Other Yalies: Bill and Hillary Clinton, actress Jodie Foster, and composer Cole Porter.

⟨⟨⟨ ELIA ⟩⟩⟩

THE PEOPLE

The films of director Elia Kazan include *East of Eden, On the Waterfront,* and *A Streetcar Named Desire.* Elia was the pen name of nineteenth-century British essayist Charles Lamb.

⟨⟨⟨ ELIE ⟩⟩⟩

THE FIRST NAME

Author and political activist Elie Wiesel received the 1986 Nobel Peace Prize. There's also Lebanese fashion designer Saab and composer Siegmeister.

⟨⟨⟨ ELIOT ⟩⟩⟩

THE LAST NAME

The works of writer T. S. Eliot (recipient of the 1948 Nobel Prize in Literature) include *Ash Wednesday*, *The Waste Land*, "The Love Song of J. Alfred Prufrock," and a collection of light verse that was the basis for the Andrew Lloyd Webber musical *Cats*. George Eliot was the pen name of nineteenth-century British novelist Mary Ann Evans, whose best-known works include *Adam Bede*, *Middlemarch*, and *Silas Marner*.

THE FIRST NAME

Eliot Ness led the Chicago team of law-enforcement agents known as "The Untouchables," who were responsible for sending gangster Al Capone to prison. Ness was portrayed by Robert Stack in the TV series *The Untouchables*, and by Kevin Costner in the film of the same name. Eliot Janeway was an American economist.

⟨⟨⟨ ELITE ⟩⟩⟩

THE SELECT

As a synonym for "high-class," commonly seen adjective clues include "Aristocratic," "Choice," "Posh," "Ritzy," and "Top drawer." In the noun form: "A-list," "Bluebloods," "Cream of the crop," "Influential group," "Upper crust," and "Who's who."

THE TYPEFACE

Elite and pica were two popular typewriter typefaces.

⟨⟨⟨ ELK ⟩⟩⟩

THE BEAST

The antlered American elk (a.k.a. wapiti) is a member of the deer family (thus a cousin to the caribou and moose) native to the western part of the U.S., including Yellowstone National Park.

THE MAN

An Elk is any member of the Benevolent and Protective Order of Elks fraternal lodge, BPOE for short.

———⟨⟨⟨ **ELKE** ⟩⟩⟩———

THE ACTRESS

The only well-known Elke is actress Sommer, whose best-known films are *The Oscar* and *A Shot in the Dark*.

———⟨⟨⟨ **ELL** ⟩⟩⟩———

THE SHAPE

L-shaped items known as ells include wings, annexes of buildings, and plumbing pipes.

THE LETTER

ELL may also be defined as the spelled-out version of the letter itself, in clues like "Kay follower" or "Em preceder."

———⟨⟨⟨ **ELLA** ⟩⟩⟩———

THE NAME

Jazz singer Fitzgerald is by far the most frequently seen Ella in crossword clues. There are also one-time Connecticut governor Grasso, actress Raines, and poet Ella Wheeler Wilcox.

THE FOREIGN WORD

"*Ella*" is the Spanish and Italian word for "she."

Not So Fast!

"Greek god": _ R _ S

EROS was the Greek god of love; ARES the Greek god of war.

<<< **ELLEN** >>>

THE NAME

There are actresses Barkin and Burstyn, TV talk-show host De-Generes, and novelist Glasgow. In the Margaret Mitchell novel *Gone With the Wind*, Scarlett O'Hara's mother is named Ellen.

<<< **ELM** >>>

THE SHADE TREE

The American elm is the state tree of Massachusetts. Dutch elm disease is a fungal ailment of elms. The "slippery elm" variety gets its name from its inner bark.

THE STREET

Elm is a popular street name. In particular, it is the setting of the *Nightmare on Elm Street* film series, whose evil main character is Freddy Krueger.

<<< **ELMO** >>>

THE NAME

Elmo is the name of a red Muppet; the "Tickle Me Elmo" doll

was America's top fad toy of 1996. Elmo is the patron saint of sailors, from whose name is derived "St. Elmo's fire." Elmo Tuttle is the bratty neighbor of the Bumsteads in the comic strip *Blondie*.

◀◀◀ ELO ▶▶▶

THE BRITISH ROCK BAND

ELO is short for Electric Light Orchestra, which was led by Jeff Lynne. Its best-known tunes were "Evil Woman," "Hold on Tight," and "Telephone Line." ELO's music is featured in the 1980 film *Xanadu*.

◀◀◀ ELOPE ▶▶▶

THE VERB

Commonly seen clues are all variations of "Avoid a big wedding," "Marry in haste," and "Run off for romance."

◀◀◀ ELS ▶▶▶

THE GOLFER

South African pro Ernie Els (pronounced "else") is nicknamed "The Big Easy" for his height and seemingly effortless swing.

THE TRAINS

This "els" is short for "elevated railways," part of the public transportation system of Chicago.

THE LETTERS

ELS may also be defined as the spelled-out version of the letter itself, in clues like "Kay followers" or "Em preceders."

<<< **ELSA** >>>

THE NAME

There's supermodel Benitez, actress Lanchester, jewelry designer Peretti, and fashion designer Schiaparelli. Characters named Elsa include the princess in the Wagner opera *Lohengrin* and the lioness in Joy Adamson's book *Born Free* and the film adaptation of the same name.

<<< **ELSE** >>>

THE ADVERB

Commonly seen clues: "Alternatively," "If not," "Otherwise," and "Ultimatum ender" (as in " . . . or else!").

THE ADJECTIVE

As an adjective, "else" is synonymous with "additional" or "more," as in "What else is new?"

<<< **ELSIE** >>>

THE MOOER

Elsie the Cow is the corporate symbol of the Borden dairy products company.

<<< **ELTON** >>>

THE MUSIC MEGASTAR

Rock singer/songwriter Elton John is one of the most successful recording artists of all time. Some of his many song hits include "Candle in the Wind," "Crocodile Rock," "Daniel," and "Rocket Man." He collaborated with Tim Rice on the scores for the Broadway musicals *The Lion King* and *Aida*.

─────── <<< **ELY** >>> ───────

THE PEOPLE

Actor Ron Ely (a dedicated crossword fan, by the way) portrayed Tarzan in a 1960s TV series and was the host of the Miss America Pageant for a time in the 1980s. Joe Ely is a country singer. Ely Culbertson was an expert on contract bridge.

THE PLACES

Ely is the name of a city in Nevada and a cathedral city in East Cambridgeshire, England.

─────── <<< **EMCEE** >>> ───────

THE NOUN/VERB

Commonly seen clues: "Game show host," "Intro giver," "Officiate at a banquet," and "Toastmaster."

─────── <<< **EMIL** >>> ───────

THE MEN

Emil Gilels was a Russian pianist. Emil Jannings won the first Best Actor Academy Award for 1928. Emil Nolde was a German painter. Czech runner Zátopek won three Olympic gold medals in 1952.

─────── <<< **EMILE** >>> ───────

THE NAME

There's French author Zola, the title character in a book by Jean-Jacques Rousseau, and the lead male character in the Rodgers and Hammerstein musical *South Pacific*.

<<< **EMIR** >>>

THE TITLE

Emir is an Arabic title given to the head of state in certain Mideast nations, such as Kuwait, Dubai, and Qatar.

INSIDER'S TIP: AMIR is also an acceptable spelling of the word, but it appears in crosswords less than one-tenth as often as EMIR.

<<< **EMIT** >>>

THE VERB

Commonly seen clues: "Discharge," "Give off," "Radiate," and "Send out."

<<< **EMMA** >>>

FOR REAL

There's poet Lazarus (who wrote "The New Colossus," inscribed at the base of the Statue of Liberty), TV actress Samms (of *Dynasty*), and film actress Thompson.

IN FICTION

Emma is a novel by Jane Austen; the title character was portrayed by Gwyneth Paltrow in the film version. Emma is the first name of the title character of the Flaubert novel *Madame Bovary*. Emma Peel is a character in the TV series *The Avengers*, portrayed by Diana Rigg. Uma Thurman portrayed Ms. Peel in the film adaptation.

<<< **EMOTE** >>>

THE VERB

Commonly seen clues: "Act poorly," "Chew the scenery," "Ham

it up," and "Overact." Although the dictionary says that the word can mean "to feign emotion" as well as to overact, the former sense is almost never cited in crosswords.

≪≪ EMS ≫≫

ON THE PAGE
Ems are measures of width in printing and typesetting, derived from the width of the letter "M." An em dash is thus longer than an en dash.

THE ABBREVIATION
The letters EMS, short for "emergency medical service," may be seen on ambulances.

ON THE MAP
Bad Ems is a spa city in Germany. The Ems River flows through Germany and the Netherlands.

THE LETTERS THEMSELVES
Clues like "Common letters" and "Mommy's triplets" refer to the multiple Ms in each word.

≪≪ EMU ≫≫

THE BIRD
The emu, related to the ostrich, is a large flightless bird native to Australia. It lays green eggs and can reach speeds of up to thirty-five miles per hour.

≪≪ ENACT ≫≫

THE VERB
Commonly seen clues: "Approve formally," "Make into law," and "Pass, as legislation."

----------- <<< **END** >>> -----------

TO CONCLUDE

Commonly seen verb clues: "Cease," "Finish," "Stop," and "Wrap up."

THE CONCLUSION

Commonly seen noun clues: "Finale," "Goal," "Outcome," "Swan song," and "Terminal."

IN SPORTS

An end is a position on a football team, as well as a wicket in the game of cricket.

----------- <<< **ENE** >>> -----------

THE ABBREVIATION

ENE stands for the direction of east-northeast, which is the point opposite west-southwest (WSW) on a compass. You'll often see city clues like "Toronto-to-Montreal dir.," where the second city is located east-northeast of the first. ENE and all the other compass points can be seen in weather reports (referring to wind direction) and on the screens of GPS devices.

THE SUFFIX

-ENE is a suffix for the name of organic compounds such as ethylene and butylene.

----------- <<< **ENERO** >>> -----------

THE MONTH

"*Enero*" is the Spanish word for "January," often clued in reference to the month that precedes it (*diciembre*) or follows it (*febrero*), as the start of the year (*el año*) or the first page of a yearly calendar (*calendario*).

---◄◄◄ **ENG** ►►►---

THE ABBREVIATIONS

As a short form of "England," commonly seen clues include: "London's loc.," "Neighbor of Scot.," and "Part of the U.K." As a short form of "English": "College dept.," "H.S. course," and "Part of E.S.L." (English as a second language).

THE NAME

Eng Bunker and his brother Chang were the original Siamese twins, from whom the term was derived.

---◄◄◄ **ENID** ►►►---

ON THE MAP

The city of Enid, Oklahoma, on the Chisholm Trail, is the site of Phillips University and Vance Air Force Base.

THE NAME

Enid Bagnold and Enid Blyton were both British writers. Enid,

Not So Fast!

"Former Italian money": L I R _

The answer can be LIRA (singular) or LIRE (plural).

the wife of Sir Geraint in the legendary tales of King Arthur, is a character in Tennyson's *Idylls of the King*.

<<< **ENOLA** >>>

THE PLANE

Enola Gay was the American warplane that carried the atomic bomb that was dropped on Hiroshima in August 1945. The plane was named for the mother of the pilot, Paul Tibbets.

<<< **ENOS** >>>

THE NAME

In the book of Genesis, Enos is the son of Seth and grandson of Adam and Eve. Enos Slaughter is a member of the Baseball Hall of Fame. Enos is a deputy sheriff in the TV series *The Dukes of Hazzard*; the series *Enos* was spun off from it. A chimpanzee named Enos was launched into space by NASA in 1961.

<<< **ENS** >>>

ON THE PAGE

Ens are a measure of width in printing and typesetting, derived from the width of the letter "N." An en dash is thus shorter than an em dash.

THE ABBREVIATION

ENS is the short form for "ensign," the lowest rank of commissioned officer in the U.S. Navy and Coast Guard. Graduates of the U.S. Naval Academy (USNA) and Coast Guard Academy (USCGA) are commissioned as ensigns.

THE LETTERS THEMSELVES

Clues like "Half of nine" and "Winning trio" refer to the multiple Ns in each word.

———— <<< ENT >>> ————

THE SUFFIX

Words to which -ENT can be added to form adjectives include "absorb," "depend," "differ," and "persist."

THE CREATURE

In Tolkien's *Lord of the Rings*, Ents are a race of humanlike trees.

THE ABBREVIATION

Clues like "Med. specialty" refer to the short form for "ear, nose, and throat."

———— <<< ENTER >>> ————

THE VERB

Commonly seen clues: "Come in," "Gain access to," "Go on stage," "Maze marking," and "Type in."

THE KEY WORD

"Enter" is a key on computer keyboards, located near the Shift key.

———— <<< ENTRE >>> ————

IN FRANCE

Entre is the French word for "between." The idiom *entre nous* (literally "between us") means "confidentially."

---<<< **EON** >>>---

A LONG TIME

In astronomy, an eon is one billion years. It is also a nonspecific unit of geologic time. Unscientifically, it is an extremely long period of time, with clues similar to "Many millennia," "Seemingly forever," and "Zillions of years."

---<<< **EPA** >>>---

THE AGENCY

EPA is short for the U.S. government's Environmental Protection Agency, established in 1970, and responsible for protecting public health and the environment. It disseminates fuel-economy stats (measured in miles per gallon, or MPG) for new automobiles, and administers the Superfund and Clean Air Act.

---<<< **EPEE** >>>---

THE WEAPON

An épée is a fencing sword, used in Olympic competition as part of the modern pentathlon.

---<<< **EPIC** >>>---

THE BIG DEAL

Clued as an adjective, you'll see "Grand-scale," "Heroic," "Larger-than-life," and "Monumental." As a noun, it's a grand-scale novel, film, etc. Director Cecil B. DeMille was noted for his film epics. Homer's *Iliad* and *Odyssey*, Dante's *Divine Comedy*, and Tolkien's *Lord of the Rings* are all considered epics.

────── <<< **ERA** >>> ──────

THE TIME

As a synonym for "significant period," commonly seen clues include "Chapter of history," "Epoch," and "Noteworthy time." You'll see specific historical eras as fill-in-the-blanks, such as "Big Band __" and "Elizabethan __." An era is also a unit of geologic time, such as the Mesozoic or Paleozoic.

THE STAT

In baseball, ERA is short for "earned-run average," an important statistic in gauging a pitcher's effectiveness.

THE AMENDMENT

ERA, short for Equal Rights Amendment, is a proposed amendment to the U.S. Constitution, intended to give equal rights to men and women, that has never been ratified.

IN THE WASH

Era is a Procter and Gamble brand of laundry detergent. It's usually clued in terms of its competitors, which include All, Fab, Surf, Tide, and Wisk.

────── <<< **ERASE** >>> ──────

THE VERB

Commonly seen clues: "Clear, as a blackboard," "Delete," "Expunge," "Obliterate," "Rub out," and "Wipe clean."

────── <<< **ERATO** >>> ──────

THE MUSE

In Greek mythology, Erato was the Muse of love poetry. Her sisters were the other eight Muses: Calliope, Clio, Euterpe, Melpomene, Polyhymnia, Terpsichore, Thalia, and Urania.

⧼⧼⧼ ERE ⧽⧽⧽

THE PREPOSITION

"Ere" is a poetic synonym of "before." It's a palindrome, since it is spelled the same in either direction. "Afore" is a poetic synonym.

⧼⧼⧼ ERECT ⧽⧽⧽

THE VERB

Commonly seen verb clues: "Build," "Construct," "Raise," and "Set up."

THE ADJECTIVE

In this sense, there's "At attention," "Not slouching," "Standing," and "Upright."

⧼⧼⧼ EREI ⧽⧽⧽

THE PALINDROME PART

ERE I is almost always clued as part of the Napoleonic palindrome "Able was I ere I saw Elba."

⧼⧼⧼ ERG ⧽⧽⧽

IN PHYSICS

An erg is a unit of work or energy, one ten-millionth of a joule.

⧼⧼⧼ ERIC ⧽⧽⧽

THE PEOPLE

There's author Ambler, actor Bana, rock guitarist Clapton, Olym-

pic skater Heiden, comic Idle, lexicographer Partridge, TV newsman Sevareid, and ancient explorer Eric the Red (father of Leif
Ericson).

INSIDER'S TIP: ERIC and ERIK are both acceptable spellings for the
ancient explorer, so be careful.

─────────── <<< **ERICA** >>> ───────────

THE PEOPLE

Nearly all crossword clues refer to just two Ericas: author Jong
and Susan Lucci's role on the soap opera *All My Children*.

─────────── <<< **ERIE** >>> ───────────

THE LAKE

Erie is the world's tenth largest lake. Of the five Great Lakes, Erie
is the shallowest, southernmost, warmest, the last discovered by
the French explorers in the seventeenth century, and the small-
est by volume. Cities on its shores include Buffalo, New York;
Erie, Pennsylvania (see below), and Toledo, Sandusky, and Cleveland, Ohio. It was the site of an 1813 battle (in the War of 1812) in
which a U.S. Navy fleet led by Commodore Oliver Perry defeated
six vessels of the British Royal Navy.

THE PENNSYLVANIA CONNECTION

The city of Erie, seat of Erie County, is located in the northwest
corner of the state on the southern shore of Lake Erie. The 1996
film *that thing you do!*, the first feature film directed by Tom
Hanks, is set in Erie.

THE CANAL

The 1825 completion of New York's Erie Canal, linking the Great

Lakes with the Atlantic Ocean, was instrumental in earning New York its "Empire State" nickname. Pejoratively dubbed "Clinton's Big Ditch," after New York governor DeWitt Clinton, who supported the funding of its construction.

THE NATIVE AMERICANS

All of the above Eries are ultimately named for the Erie Indians, who once inhabited the southern shore of Lake Erie. The tribe was exterminated by and absorbed into the Iroquois circa 1600, for aiding the Hurons, an enemy of the Iroquois League.

INSIDER'S TIP: ERIE is the only Great Lake whose name has four letters, and HURON is the only five-letter Great Lake, so you can safely ignore the rest of any other four-letter or five-letter "Great Lake" clue and fill in the answer PDQ (or ASAP, if you prefer).

⟨⟨⟨ **ERIK** ⟩⟩⟩

THE PEOPLE

In real life, there's actor Estrada and French composer Satie. Erik is the title character in *Phantom of the Opera* and a hunter in the Wagner opera *The Flying Dutchman*.

⟨⟨⟨ **ERIN** ⟩⟩⟩

THE COUNTRY

"Erin" is a literary synonym for Ireland, a.k.a. "Hibernia" and "The Emerald Isle." It's the homeland of writers James Joyce and William Yeats. The patriotic phrase *"Erin go bragh"* means "Ireland forever."

THE NAME

Actress Erin Moran appeared on the sitcom *Happy Days*. Julia

> ## *Not So Fast!*
>
> "String tie": B O L _
>
> *Both BOLO and BOLA are correct.*

Roberts won an Academy Award for portraying the title character in the film *Erin Brockovich*. Erin is also the name of one of the daughters in the TV series *The Waltons*.

<<< ERLE >>>

THE AUTHOR

Erle Stanley Gardner created the lawyer/sleuth Perry Mason and his assistant Della Street. You'll see "first-name" clues such as "Agatha's colleague" (for Agatha Christie), that may also reference Gardner's other literary contemporaries, such as Rex Stout or Dashiell Hammett.

<<< ERMA >>>

THE AUTHOR

The writings of Erma Bombeck take a humorous look at suburban life. Her syndicated column was "At Wit's End." The clue "Cope Book aunt" refers to Bombeck's *Aunt Erma's Cope Book*.

<<< ERN >>>

THE SUFFIX

As a "directional" suffix, -ERN can be added to "north," "south," "east," and "west."

THE BIRD

ERN is an alternative spelling of ERNE (see below).

—————— <<< **ERNE** >>> ——————

THE BIRD

An erne is a white-tailed sea eagle that feeds on fish.

—————— <<< **ERNIE** >>> ——————

REAL

There's baseball Hall of Famer Banks, golf pro Els, singer "Tennessee" Ernie Ford, comedian Kovacs, and World War II correspondent Pyle.

FICTIONAL

Muppet Ernie is Bert's friend on the kids' TV series *Sesame Street*. Ernie is one of the elves seen in commercials for Keebler cookies. It's the first name of Sergeant Bilko, the conniving character in the 1950s sitcom *The Phil Silvers Show*, portrayed by Silvers. And Ernie is one of the sons on the 1960s sitcom *My Three Sons*.

—————— <<< **ERODE** >>> ——————

THE VERB

Commonly seen clues are variations on "Eat into," "Undermine," and "Wear away."

—————— <<< **EROS** >>> ——————

THE GOD

Youngest of the Greek gods, winged archer Eros was the son of

Aphrodite and Zeus, and the god of love. His Roman equivalent is Cupid, a.k.a. Amor.

THE STATUE

Atop the memorial fountain in London's Piccadilly Circus is the statue formally named *The Angel of Christian Charity*, but popularly called *Eros*.

THE ASTEROID

Discovered in 1898, this Eros is the second largest of the near-Earth asteroids.

———— <<< **ERR** >>> ————

THE VERB

Commonly seen clues: "Flub," "Go wrong," "Goof," "Make a mistake," "Mess up," and "Slip." "To err is human" is a line from English writer Alexander Pope.

———— <<< **ERROR** >>> ————

THE NOUN

Commonly seen clues: "Baseball blunder," "Boo-boo," "Glitch," "Goof," "Miscue," and "Mistake."

———— <<< **ERS** >>> ————

THE ABBREVIATION

As a short form of "emergency rooms," commonly seen clues are variations of "Hosp. areas," "Trauma ctrs.," and "Where MDs work."

THE SOUNDS

As the sounds made by a hesitant speaker, there's "Pause fillers," "Speech stumbles," and "Verbal uncertainties."

INSIDER'S TIP: Many of the medical clues for ERS may also apply to ORS (short for "operating rooms"), so be careful.

<<< **ERST** >>>

THE OLD-TIME ADVERB

An archaic term for "once" or "formerly," it is seen today mostly as part of the word "erstwhile."

<<< **ERTE** >>>

THE ARTIST

Russian-born artist Erté is remembered for his Art Deco works, including many illustrations for the magazine *Harper's Bazaar*.

<<< **ESAU** >>>

IN THE BIBLE

In the book of Genesis, Esau was the son of Isaac and the twin brother of Jacob.

<<< **ESE** >>>

THE ABBREVIATION

ESE stands for the direction of east-southeast, which is the point opposite west-northwest (WNW) on a compass. You'll often see city clues like "Pittsburgh-to-Baltimore dir.," where the second city is located east-southeast of the first. ESE and all the other compass points can be seen in weather reports (referring to wind direction) and on the screens of GPS devices.

THE SUFFIX

Words ending in -ESE are usually either real languages/nationalities (like Japanese and Portuguese) or the jargon/accent of a particular region (such as Brooklynese) or profession (such as "legalese").

———<<< **ESP** >>>———

THE ABBREVIATION

As a short form of "extrasensory perception," commonly seen clues include "Clairvoyance, for short," "Mentalist's claim," "Paranormal power," "Psychic's skill," "Sixth sense," and "Uncommon sense."

———<<< **ESPY** >>>———

THE VERB

As a synonym for "notice," commonly seen clues include "Catch sight of," "Lay eyes on," and "Spot."

THE AWARD

The ESPY Awards are presented annually by the ESPN cable network for achievements in various sports.

———<<< **ESS** >>>———

THE SHAPE

Commonly seen clues: "Part of a winding road," "Pothook shape," "Serpentine shape," and "Slalom curve."

THE LETTER

"Double-curve letter," "Superman's insignia," "Tee preceder," and "The first of September" all clue the spelled-out version of the letter S.

THE SUFFIX

-ESS is a feminine suffix, but not exactly politically correct these days in terms for people.

<<< **ESSE** >>>

TO CAESAR

Esse is Latin for "to be" or "existence." The idiom *in esse* means "actually." It's the first word of the Latin motto of North Carolina.

<<< **ESSEN** >>>

ON THE MAP

The German city of Essen, in the Ruhr Valley, was formerly a center for the coal-mining and steelmaking industries.

<<< **ESSO** >>>

THE BRAND

Esso, short for "Standard Oil," is the former name of the Exxon oil company, and the brand of gasoline it sold. The Esso brand is still used at Canadian gas stations. It is often defined as the competitor of other defunct U.S. gasoline brand names, such as Flying "A."

———————<<< **EST** >>>———————

THE ABBREVIATIONS

As a short form for "estimate," you'll see clues like "Approx." and "Ballpark fig." When it stands for "Eastern Standard Time," the clue will usually have an abbreviated state or city name, like "D.C. clock setting" or "N.C. winter hours." If it's short for "established," there's "Cornerstone abbr." and "Founded, for short."

THE SUFFIXES

-EST is a superlative suffix for adjectives as well as an archaic or Biblical suffix for verbs.

THE FOREIGN WORDS

Est means "is" in both French (as in *"C'est la vie"*) and Latin (as in *"id est,"* the spelled-out version of "i.e.," which means "that is").

———————<<< **ESTA** >>>———————

IN SPANISH

Spelled *"está,"* it means "is" or "are," as in *"Cómo está usted?"* ("How are you?"). Without the accent mark, it means "this."

Not So Fast!

"Exited": _ E _ T

The answer can be LEFT or the nearly synonymous WENT.

Either meaning may be seen in crosswords, since accent marks are omitted from the answers in American crosswords.

<<< ESTATE >>>

THE NOUN

An estate may be bequeathed property or a large property with an elaborate house.

<<< ESTE >>>

IN ITALY

Este is an Italian town near Padua. An Italian noble family took its surname from the town. The Villa d'Este is a tourist attraction in Tivoli, near Rome.

IN SPANISH

"Este" is the Spanish word for "east." Punta del Este is a resort region in Uruguay.

<<< ESTEE >>>

THE NAME

Estée Lauder founded the cosmetics company that bears her name.

<<< ESTER >>>

IN CHEMISTRY

An ester is a compound that results from an acid reacting with an alcohol. Often aromatic, esters are used in perfume manufacture. Examples of esters are triglyceride, banana oil, and any acetate compound.

⋖⋖⋖ **ESTES** ⋗⋗⋗

THE PEOPLE

Actor Rob Estes appeared on the TV series *Melrose Place*. Simon Estes is an operatic bass-baritone. Tennessee senator Estes Kefauver was Adlai Stevenson's vice presidential running mate in the election of 1956.

THE PLACE

The resort town of Estes Park, Colorado, is the headquarters for Rocky Mountain National Park.

⋖⋖⋖ **ETA** ⋗⋗⋗

THE LETTER

The vowel eta is the seventh letter of the Greek alphabet, preceded by zeta and followed by theta. An uppercase eta resembles the letter "H."

THE ABBREVIATION

As a short form of "estimated time of arrival," commonly seen clues are variations of "Airport stat.," "LAX posting" (LAX is the symbol for Los Angeles International Airport), or "Pilot's announcement."

INSIDER'S TIP: ETD (short for "estimated time of departure") may also be a possible answer to many of the clues for ETA, although the latter appears much more often in crosswords.

⋘ **ETAL** ⋙

THE ABBREVIATION

"Et al." is a short form for the Latin *et alii* or *et alia* ("and others").
It is frequently used in footnotes and bibliographies to shorten a
long list of names.

⋘ **ETAT** ⋙

IN FRANCE

État is the French word for "state." A coup d'état is a sudden over-
throw of a government. Louis XIV once said, *"L'état, c'est moi"* ("I
am the state").

⋘ **ETC** ⋙

THE ABBREVIATION

Commonly seen clues are variations of "And so on: Abbr.,"
"Catchall abbr.," and "List shortener."

⋘ **ETCH** ⋙

THE VERB

Commonly seen clues: "Draw on glass," "Engrave deeply," "Out-
line clearly," and "Work with acid."

⋘ **ETE** ⋙

IN FRANCE

"Été" is the French word for "summer." It is preceded by *print-
emps* (spring) and followed by *automne* (autumn).

———————— <<< **ETES** >>> ————————

THE FRENCH VERB

In addition to the French plural for "summer," *êtes* (spelled with different accent marks) is French for "are." *Vous êtes* means "you are."

———————— <<< **ETH** >>> ————————

THE SUFFIXES

The names of ordinal numbers whose cardinal forms end in "Y," such as "twentieth" and "fiftieth," end in -ETH. ETH is also an archaic/Biblical verb suffix, as in "leadeth" and "maketh."

ON THE MAP

"Eth." is an abbreviation for the African nation of Ethiopia, whose capital is Addis Ababa and whose neighboring countries are Eritrea, Djibouti, Kenya, Somalia, and Sudan.

———————— <<< **ETHAN** >>> ————————

REAL

Vermonter Ethan Allen led the Green Mountain Boys during the American Revolution. Ethan Coen is one of the two moviemaking Coen brothers (the other is Joel). Actor Ethan Hawke is an ex-husband of actress Uma Thurman.

FICTIONAL

Ethan Frome is a novel by Edith Wharton. Ethan Hunt is Tom Cruise's role in the *Mission: Impossible* film series.

Need to Know: Crossword Latin 101

The 20 Latin words that appear most often as crossword answers:

ala (wing, plural is *alae*)

alia (others, also *alii*)

amas (you love)

amat (he loves, she loves)

amo (I love)

amor (love)

ars (art)

ave (hello)

avis (bird, plural is *aves*)

dea (goddess)

dei (gods)

diem (day)

ecce (behold)

esse (to be)

hic (here)

ora (pray, mouths)

ova (eggs)

res (thing)

sic (thus)

ursa (bear)

<<< ETHER >>>

THE NOUN

Ether is a former anesthetic, as well as a synonym for the clear sky.

<<< ETNA >>>

THE SPEWER

Italy's Mount Etna is an active volcano on the island of Sicily. Sicilians call the peak "Mongibello."

◀◀◀ ETO ▶▶▶

THE ABBREVIATION

ETO is short for "European Theater of Operations," the Allies' term for the World War II section of Europe north of Italy and the Mediterranean coast. ETO's commander was General Dwight D. Eisenhower, whose initials (DDE) are often used to clue it.

◀◀◀ ETON ▶▶▶

THE SCHOOL

Eton College is a British prep school on the Thames, founded by Henry VI in 1440. Notable people who attended Eton include Princes William and Harry, George Orwell, Percy Shelley, Ian Fleming, and Fleming's spy James Bond. Eton's rival school is Harrow.

◀◀◀ ETRE ▶▶▶

IN FRANCE

Être is the french infinitive verb for "to be." "Raison d'être" is an idiom for "justification" (literally "reason to be").

◀◀◀ ETS ▶▶▶

IN SCI-FI

As an abbreviation for "extraterrestrials," commonly seen clues are variations of "Aliens," "Little green men," "Martians, for example," and "UFO pilots."

IN SCHOOL

ETS, or Educational Testing Service, is the company that develops and administers standardized tests such as the SAT.

⟨⟨⟨ ETTA ⟩⟩⟩

REAL

There's editorial cartoonist Hulme, singers Etta James and Etta Jones, and Etta Place, girlfriend of the Sundance Kid, partner in crime of Butch Cassidy. Place is portrayed by Katharine Ross in the film *Butch Cassidy and the Sundance Kid*.

FICTIONAL

The old comic strip *Etta Kett* was designed to teach good manners to children ("etiquette," get it?).

⟨⟨⟨ ETTE ⟩⟩⟩

THE SUFFIX

-ETTE can denote miniaturization (as in "kitchenette"), feminization (as in "bachelorette"), or imitation (as in "leatherette"). Other "Suffix for" words often seen are disk, luncheon, major, and novel.

⟨⟨⟨ ETTU ⟩⟩⟩

THE ACCUSATION

In the Shakespeare play *Julius Caesar*, "Et tu, Brute?" (Latin for "You too, Brutus?") are among the last words spoken by the title character to Brutus, one of his assassins.

⟨⟨⟨ EVA ⟩⟩⟩

THE ACTRESSES

There's Gabor (sister of Zsa Zsa) of the 1960s sitcom *Green Acres*, Longoria Parker of the TV series *Desperate Housewives*, Mendes of *Training Day,* and Marie Saint of the Hitchcock film *North by Northwest.*

OTHER PEOPLE

Argentine first lady Eva (a.k.a. Evita) Perón, wife of Juan, was portrayed by Madonna in the film version of the Andrew Lloyd Webber musical *Evita.* Little Eva is a character in the Harriet Beecher Stowe novel *Uncle Tom's Cabin.* And Eva is the heroine of the Richard Wagner opera *Die Meistersinger.*

THE ACRONYM

To NASA, EVA stands for "extravehicular activity," its term for a spacewalk.

--------- <<< **EVAN** >>> ---------

THE NAME

There's Indiana politician Bayh, author Connell, and author Hunter. Evan is the Welsh equivalent of the name John. The 2007 film *Evan Almighty* stars Steve Carell as the title character.

--------- <<< **EVE** >>> ---------

THE DAY BEFORE

Commonly seen clues in this sense: "Celebratory night," "Holiday preceder," and "December 24 or 31."

THE PEOPLE

Eve is the first woman mentioned in the Bible, mother of Cain, Abel, and Seth, and spouse of Adam. Title characters named Eve are portrayed by Anne Baxter in the 1950 film *All About Eve* and Joanne Woodward in the 1957 film *The Three Faces of Eve.* Actress Eve Arden had the title role in the 1950s sitcom *Our Miss Brooks*.

———— <<< **EVEL** >>> ————

THE NAME

Professional daredevil Evel Knievel was noted for his motorcycle stunts.

———— <<< **EVEN** >>> ————

MOSTLY IN BALANCE

Usually clued as an adjective, there's "Balanced," "Level," "Neck and neck," "Not odd" (as a number), "Tied," and "Uniform." When clued as a verb, it's "Equalize" or "Smooth out."

———— <<< **EVENT** >>> ————

THE NOUN

Commonly seen clues: "Happening," "Important occasion," "Occurrence," and "Track-meet contest." Olympic events include the ten-event decathlon, high jump, javelin, marathon, and shot put.

Not So Fast!

"Shopping center": M A _ _

The answer can be MALL or MART.

——— <<< **EVER** >>> ———

THE ADVERB
Commonly seen clues: "Always," "At any time," "Continuously," "Even once," and "In any way."

——— <<< **EVES** >>> ———

THE BOOK
Besides the plural of the time or the name, *Eve's Diary* is a book by Mark Twain.

——— <<< **EVIL** >>> ———

THE BAD
Commonly seen clues: "Diabolical," "Satanic," "Sinful," and "Wicked." Dr. Evil is one of Mike Myers's roles in the *Austin Powers* film series.

——— <<< **EWE** >>> ———

THE BEAST
Clues for the female sheep are variations of "Flock member," "Lamb's mother," "Ram's mate," and "Wool source."

——— <<< **EWER** >>> ———

HOLDING WATER
A ewer is a wide-spouted water pitcher.

——— <<< **EXIT** >>> ———

THE VERB
Commonly seen verb clues: "Depart," "Go," "Leave the stage," and "Take off."

THE NOUN

Noun clues: "Door sign," "Escape route," "Highway ramp," and "Way out."

―――――⟨⟨⟨ **EYE** ⟩⟩⟩―――――

THE VERB

Commonly seen verb clues: "Examine," "Ogle," "Look at," and "Observe."

THE NOUN

Noun clues: "CBS logo," "Hurricane center," "Needle hole," and "Potato part."

―――――⟨⟨⟨ **EYRE** ⟩⟩⟩―――――

THE CHARACTER

Jane Eyre, title character of the Jane Austen novel, is the governess of Thornfield Hall, the English manor of Edward Rochester, whom she eventually marries.

―――――⟨⟨⟨ **EZRA** ⟩⟩⟩―――――

THE NAME

The Old Testament book of Ezra follows II Chronicles and precedes Nehemiah. Philanthropist Ezra Cornell co-founded the Ivy League university named for him; Ezra Pound was an American-born poet.

MATA HARI, C. 1910.
(LIBRARY OF CONGRESS)

the
LETTERS
F—H

<<< **FEE** >>>

THE NOUN

Commonly seen clues: "Commission, for example," "Honorarium," "Professional payment," and "Service charge."

<<< **FLO** >>>

THE NAME

Florenz "Flo" Ziegfeld was a Broadway showman. Mel's Diner waitress Flo Castleberry is a character in the sitcom *Alice*, portrayed by Polly Holliday. Flo is also the wife of the title character in the comic strip *Andy Capp*.

<<< **GALA** >>>

THE PARTY

Commonly seen clues: "Big bash," "Celebration," "Festive occasion," and "Shindig." GALA may also be an adjective, with clues like "Festive."

<<< **GAS** >>>

IN CHEMISTRY

Gaseous chemical elements include argon, helium, hydrogen, krypton, neon, nitrogen, oxygen, radon, and xenon.

IN YOUR CAR

As a short form for "gasoline," there's "Auto fuel," "Driver's need," "Highway sign," and "Tank filler." "Gas" is also a slang term for a car's accelerator pedal.

FIGURATIVELY SPEAKING

As a synonym for "empty talk," commonly seen clues include

"Blather," "Hot air," and "Idle chatter." When it means "something entertaining," there's "Loads of fun" and "Swell time."

<<< **GEE** >>>

THE EXCLAMATION

"Golly!," "That's amazing!," "Wow!," and "You don't say!" are all exclamations of amazement like GEE.

THE LETTER

As the spelled-out version of the letter G, you may see wordplay clues like "Capital of Germany." GEE is a slang term for $1,000 (G being short for "grand"), with clues like "Thou" and "Ten C-notes."

<<< **GEM** >>>

LITERALLY SPEAKING

"Precious stone," "Jewel," and "Sparkler" clue a gemstone in general. Types of gems include diamond, emerald, opal, ruby, sapphire, topaz, and turquoise.

FIGURATIVELY SPEAKING

As a person or thing that is highly prized, there's "Masterpiece," "Rare find," and "Special person."

<<< **GENE** >>>

IN SCIENCE

As the unit of heredity, commonly seen clues include "Chromosome component," "Inheritance factor," "Splicer's need," and "Trait transmitter."

THE NAME

There's Oscar actor Hackman, screen dancer Kelly, jazz drummer Krupa, and comic actor Wilder.

<<< **GERE** >>>

THE MAN

The films of actor Richard Gere include *Chicago, I'm Not There, The Cotton Club, An Officer and a Gentleman, Pretty Woman, Primal Fear,* and *Runaway Bride.*

<<< **GLEE** >>>

THE FEELING

Commonly seen clues: "Elation," "Happiness," "High spirits," "Jubilation," and "Merriment."

<<< **GNAT** >>>

THE BUG

The pesky, biting insect is actually a small fly.

<<< **GTO** >>>

THE WHEELS

The Pontiac GTO "muscle car" was made in the 1960s and

Not So Fast!

"Mortgage, for example": L _ _ N

The answer can be LOAN or LIEN.

1970s, and revived by General Motors in 2004–2006. The 1964 tune "GTO" by Ronny and the Daytonas is about the car.

‹‹‹ HAHA ›››

THE EXCLAMATION

Commonly seen clues are variations of "Reaction to a joke," "Sounds of laughter," and "Very funny!"

‹‹‹ HAIR ›››

THE GROWING THING

Commonly seen clues in this sense: "Barber's expertise," "Eyebrows, essentially," "Locks," and "Mane thing." Because of the narrowness of a hair, the word can also mean a narrow margin, such as of victory.

THE MUSICAL

The 1960s Broadway show *Hair* is known as "The American Tribal Love-Rock Musical." Its songs include "Aquarius" and "Easy to Be Hard."

‹‹‹ HAL ›››

THE NAME

There's song lyricist Hal David, actors Holbrook and Linden, Broadway producer Prince, and the evil computer in the film *2001: A Space Odyssey*.

‹‹‹ HALO ›››

THE LIGHT

A halo can be the circular light above an angel's head as well as the bright circle of light sometimes seen around the sun or moon. A halo is thought to be a symbol of sanctity, saintliness, or virtue.

<<< HARE >>>

IN GENERAL

A relative of the rabbit, the hare is part of the order of mammals known as lagomorphs. One may be the quarry of a fox or hound. A young hare is known as a leveret.

SPECIFICALLY

The March Hare is a character in Lewis Carroll's *Alice's Adventures in Wonderland*. A hare lost the race to the tortoise in an Aesop's fable.

<<< HARI >>>

THE SPY

The Dutch-born Mata Hari was an infamous spy during World War I. She was portrayed by Greta Garbo in a 1932 film.

<<< HAS >>>

THE VERB

Commonly seen clues: "Keeps," "Orders for dinner," "Owns," and "Possesses."

<<< HEN >>>

THE FEMALES

In addition to the egg-laying barnyard animal, a hen can also be a female lobster, octopus, pheasant, or turkey.

◀◀◀ HER ▶▶▶

THE PRONOUN

Commonly seen clues: "Part of HRH" (Her Royal Highness), "Term for a ship," "That woman," and "Yonder lass." "And I Love Her" is a Beatles tune. In the 1960s, President Lyndon Johnson had pet beagles named Him and Her.

◀◀◀ HERE ▶▶▶

THE ADVERB/EXCLAMATION

Commonly seen adverb clues: "In this place," "Now's partner," "Present," and "Roll-call answer." Grammatically speaking, using "Here!" to call a dog makes it an interjection.

◀◀◀ HERO ▶▶▶

THE BRAVE ONE

Commonly seen clues in this sense: "Idolized one," "Life saver," "Man of the hour," "Medal recipient," and "Protagonist."

THE LUNCH

A hero is a sandwich on a long roll. Other names for it are grinder, hoagie, po' boy, and sub.

IN MYTH

In Greek mythology, Hero was a priestess who loved a young man named Leander.

◀◀◀ HES ▶▶▶

THE PLURAL

Commonly seen clues: "Fellows," "Guys," "Men," and "for example" clues with male animals such as boars, bucks, bulls, roosters, and stags.

THE CONTRACTION

"He's" is almost always clued by fill-in-the-blanks, in reference to "He's a Rebel" (tune by the Crystals), "He's So Fine" (tune by the Chiffons), "For He's a Jolly Good Fellow," etc.

——— <<< **HIE** >>> ———

THE VERB

As a synonym for "move quickly," commonly seen clues include "Hurry," "Make haste," "Rush," and "Shake a leg."

——— <<< **HONE** >>> ———

THE VERB

Commonly seen clues: "Fine-tune," "Improve," "Perfect," and "Sharpen."

——— <<< **HORA** >>> ———

THE DANCE

The hora is a traditional Romanian and Israeli dance, performed in a circle.

LYRICIST IRA GERSHWIN, C. 1938. (COURTESY OF
IRA AND LEONORE GERSHWIN TRUSTS)

the
LETTER
I

<<< IAGO >>>

THE NAME

The villainous Iago is a character in the Shakespeare play *Othello*, and the Giuseppe Verdi opera based on it, *Otello*. Iago is also the name of the parrot in the Disney animated film *Aladdin*.

<<< IAN >>>

THE NAME

There's James Bond creator Fleming, actors Holm, McKellen, and McShane, and golfer Woosnam. Janis Ian is a pop singer.

<<< ICE >>>

THE HARD STUFF

Ice is a winter road hazard, a drink cooler, the surface for skaters and hockey players, a treatment for sprains, and a slang term for diamonds.

THE VERB

Besides adding icing to a cake, "ice" can mean to "make sure of" or "assure."

<<< ICON >>>

THE SYMBOLS

An icon may be a religious image, a much-admired person, or a graphic image on a computer screen.

<<< IDA >>>

THE NAME

Ida was the wife of President William McKinley. Ida Tarbell was a "muckraking" author. Ida Lupino was an actress and director. "Ida, Sweet as Apple Cider" is an old song. Fictionally speaking, *Princess Ida* is a Gilbert and Sullivan operetta, and Ida was the title character's mother on the sitcom *Rhoda*.

THE PLACES

Crete's Mount Ida was sacred in Greek mythology. "Ida." is an abbreviation for Idaho, usually defined in terms of its neighbors (British Columbia, Montana, Nevada, Oregon, Utah, Washington, and Wyoming) or its capital (Boise).

<<< **IDEA** >>>

THE NOUN

Commonly seen clues: "Brainstorm," "Creative thought," "Inspiration," and "Notion."

<<< **IDEAL** >>>

AS GOOD AS IT GETS

Commonly seen adjective clues: "Best," "Exemplary," "Perfect," and "Utopian." As a noun: "Paragon," "Role model," and "Standard of perfection."

Not So Fast!

"Football stats: Abbr.": _ D S

The answer can be TDS (short for "touchdowns") or YDS (short for "yards").

◁◁◁ IDES ▷▷▷

THE DAY

In the ancient Roman calendar, the ides was the fifteenth day of March, May, July, and October, and the thirteenth day of the other months. The ides of March was the day Julius Caesar was assassinated, as he was warned by a soothsayer in the Shakespeare play.

◁◁◁ IDI ▷▷▷

THE NAME

Idi Amin was the notorious 1970s dictator of Uganda. Forest Whitaker won an Academy Award for portraying him in the 2006 film *The Last King of Scotland*.

◁◁◁ IDLE ▷▷▷

THE ADJECTIVE AND VERB

Commonly seen adjective clues: "Doing nothing," "In neutral," "Just hanging around," and "Not working." In the verbal sense, there's "Lounge around" and "Run in neutral."

THE NAME

British comedian Eric Idle was a member of the group Monty Python, whose other members included John Cleese and Michael Palin.

◁◁◁ IDO ▷▷▷

THE AFFIRMATION

Clued most often as a nuptial response, as variations of "Altar agreement," "Bachelor's last words," "Rite answer," and "Wedding vow." "I do" is also spoken by a witness in a courtroom while being sworn in.

———————— <<< **IDOL** >>> ————————

THE NOUN

Commonly seen clues referring to a person: "Admired one," "Hero," "Object of adoration," and "One on a pedestal." Referring to an object: "False god," "Golden calf," and "Graven image." There's also the TV series *American Idol*.

———————— <<< **IGET** >>> ————————

BLANKETY-BLANKS

Partial song-title clues: "__ a Kick out of You" (Cole Porter), "__ Around" (Beach Boys), and "__ Weak" (Brenda Carlisle). In colloquial phrases: "Now __ it!" and "This is the thanks __?"

———————— <<< **IGOR** >>> ————————

THE NAME

Real Igors include helicopter inventor Sikorsky and composer Stravinsky. Igor is the traditional name of the villain's assistant in horror films, specifically in the Mel Brooks horror-film satire *Young Frankenstein*. *Prince Igor* is an opera by Alexander Borodin.

———————— <<< **III** >>> ————————

TO CAESAR

As the Roman numeral for three, III appears on ancient sundials, at the end of some men's names (meaning "the third"), and at the end of film titles, denoting the second sequel in a series.

<<< **IKE** >>>

THE NAME

Ike was the nickname of World War II general and 1950s president Dwight Eisenhower. Ike Turner was a rock musician, ex-husband of Tina. Ike Clanton was one of the bad-guy foes of the Earp brothers at the famous O.K. Corral gunfight. Ike is also the name of a boy in the *South Park* animated TV series.

<<< **ILE** >>>

IN FRANCE

"*Île*" is the French word for "island," and may be clued generically in variations of "Seine sight" and "Spot in *la mer*" (French for "the sea"). Islands owned by France include Martinique and Tahiti. Île-de-France is a French region, Île de la Cité is an island in Paris in the river Seine, and Île du Diable is the French name for Devil's Island.

THE SUFFIX

-ILE can be added to words such as "duct," "percent," and "tact."

<<< **ILIE** >>>

THE RACKET-EER

Romanian-born tennis pro Ilie Nastase was one of the world's best players in the 1970s, a rival of Bjorn Borg and Jimmy Connors.

BLANKETY-BLANK

"Would __ to you?" clues I LIE.

<<< **ILL** >>>

THE ADJECTIVE/ADVERB

Commonly seen adjective clues: "Below par," "Indisposed," "Under the weather," and "Unwell." As an adverb: "Poorly," "Unfavorably," and "Unsatisfactorily."

THE ABBREVIATION

Clues for the short form for "Illinois" may refer to its neighboring states (Indiana, Iowa, Kentucky, Missouri, and Wisconsin), cities (such as Chicago), its universities (such as Northwestern), and its residents (such as Barack Obama).

<<< **IMA** >>>

BLANKETY-BLANKS

Partial song-title clues: "__ Believer" (Monkees), "__ Little Teapot" (kid's tune), "__ Loser" (Beatles), "__ Slave 4 U" (Britney Spears), and "__ Woman" (Maria Muldaur). "I'm a Yankee Doodle Dandy" is the start of a patriotic song composed by George M. Cohan.

<<< **IMAGE** >>>

THE NOUN

In the literal sense, commonly seen clues include "Likeness," "Picture," and "Reflection." Figuratively, there's "Candidate's concern," "Public persona," and "Spin doctor's crafting."

‹‹‹ INA ›››

BLANKETY-BLANKS

"__ nutshell," "Once __ while," "One __ million," "Pig __ poke,"
"__ pig's eye!," and "Tempest __ teapot" all clue IN A.

THE NAME

Once in a while, you'll see clues that mention long-ago film actresses Ina Balin or Ina Claire.

‹‹‹ INANE ›››

THE ADJECTIVE

Commonly seen clues: "Absurd," "Nonsensical," "Pointless,"
"Preposterous," "Ridiculous," and "Silly."

‹‹‹ INCA ›››

THE PEOPLE

The Inca empire flourished in what is today the area around Cuzco, Peru, from about 1200 to 1500. The ruins of the Inca city of Machu Picchu are a tourist attraction today. The Spanish, led by Francisco Pizarro, conquered the Incas, led by Emperor Atahualpa, in 1533. *Inca Gold* is a novel by Clive Cussler.

‹‹‹ INE ›››

THE SUFFIX

-INE is a chemical suffix, an adjective suffix meaning "resembling," and can be added to words like "hero" and "serpent."

MUSICALLY SPEAKING

Tchaikovsky's Fifth Symphony and Beethoven's Seventh Sym-

> ## Not So Fast!
>
> **"Norwegian royal name":** O L A _
>
> *Both OLAV and OLAF are correct spellings.*

phony are just two of many famous works written in the key of E major, "in E" for short.

<<< INERT >>>

NOT MOVING TOO WELL

Commonly seen clues in this sense: "Listless," "Motionless," "Sluggish," and "Still."

IN CHEMISTRY

The inert gases (argon, helium, krypton, neon, radon, xenon) have little or no ability to react with other elements.

<<< INGE >>>

THE PLAYWRIGHT

The plays of William Inge include *Bus Stop, Come Back, Little Sheba,* and *Picnic.* He also wrote the screenplay for *Splendor in the Grass.*

<<< INIT >>>

THE ABBREVIATION

As a short form of "initial," commonly seen clues include "Handkerchief ltr.," "Monogram pt.," and "OK" (in the verb sense).

BLANKETY-BLANKS

Colloquialisms like "__ for the long haul" and "What's __ for me?" clue IN IT.

<<< **INK** >>>

LITERAL

Commonly seen clues: "Calligrapher's need," "Pen filler," "Prepare a press," "Print-shop purchase," and "Squid secretion."

FIGURATIVE

"Ink" is a slang term for publicity or press coverage. As a verb, it means to sign, as a contract.

<<< **INLET** >>>

ON THE MAP

An inlet is an indentation of a shoreline, a small bay or arm of the sea, or a narrow passage between islands. Synonymous terms include cove, estuary, firth, fjord, and sound.

<<< **INN** >>>

THE STOP

Commonly seen clues: "Bed-and-breakfast," "Roadhouse," "Rural hotel," "Travel-guide listing," and references to the Holiday Inn and Ramada Inn lodging chains. The sitcom *Newhart* is set at a Vermont inn.

<<< **INON** >>>

THE PHRASE

Commonly seen clues are variations of "Aware of" and "Privy

to." To "barge in on" is to interrupt, and one can "get in on the ground floor."

<<< **INRE** >>>

IN LEGALESE

"In re" appears at the beginning of legal memos, where it is synonymous with "about," "as to," "concerning," "in the matter of," and "regarding."

<<< **INS** >>>

THE PLURAL

"Ins" are current holders of political offices, who may be helpful contacts to get something done. "Ins and outs" are the particular details of something.

THE ABBREVIATIONS

INS may be short for the Immigration and Naturalization Service (which issues Green Cards to non-citizen residents) or "insurance."

<<< **INTO** >>>

THE PREPOSITION

Commonly seen clues are variations of "Division word," "Enthusiastic about," "Fascinated by," and "Fond of."

<<< **INTRO** >>>

TO START

Commonly seen clues: "Emcee's words," "Lead-in," "Opening remarks," and "Prologue."

─────── <<< **ION** >>> ───────

IN SCIENCE

An ion is an electrically charged atom or particle. Ions are propelled within a cyclotron.

ON THE ROAD

Ion is a formerly made model of the Saturn automobile.

─────── <<< **IONIA** >>> ───────

ON THE MAP

Ionia was an ancient Greek region of Asia Minor, located today in western Turkey and nearby islands in the Aegean Sea. The old city of Ephesus was located there.

─────── <<< **IOTA** >>> ───────

THE LETTER

Iota is the ninth letter of the Greek alphabet, following theta and preceding kappa.

THE BIT

As a very small quantity, commonly seen clues include "Scintilla," "Smidgen," "Tiny amount," and "Whit."

─────── <<< **IOU** >>> ───────

THE ABBREVIATION

Commonly seen clues: "Debtor's note," "Letters of credit," "Marker," and "Promise to pay."

———— <<< **IRA** >>> ————

THE FUNDS

As an abbreviation for "Individual Retirement Account," commonly seen clues include "Keogh or 401(k) alternative," "Kind of tax shelter," "Nest-egg letters," and "S&L offering."

THE NAME

There's song lyricist Gershwin (a dedicated crossword fan himself, brother of George), novelist Levin, and public radio personality Glass.

THE ORGANIZATION

IRA may also be short for the Irish Republican Army, an Irish nationalist organization.

———— <<< **IRAE** >>> ————

THE HYMN

"Dies Irae" (Latin for "Day of Wrath") is a medieval Latin hymn that is sometimes part of a Roman Catholic requiem mass.

———— <<< **IRAN** >>> ————

THE MIDDLE EAST COUNTRY

Once known as Persia, Iran's neighboring countries are Armenia, Azerbaijan, Iraq, Pakistan, Turkey, and Turkmenistan. It lies on the Caspian Sea, the Gulf of Oman, and the Persian Gulf. The modern Persian language is known to natives as Farsi. Iran is a member of the oil cartel OPEC. Many similarly worded clues may define both IRAN and IRANI (see below).

BLANKETY-BLANKS

If I Ran the Circus and *If I Ran the Zoo* are children's books by Dr. Seuss.

<<< **IRANI** >>>

THE NATIVE

IRANI may be defined in terms of its cities in clues like "Tehran resident" (other major cities are Qom, Shiraz, and Tabriz), notable citizens (such as former president Bani-Sadr, and ayatollah or shah, titles of former rulers), or rials, the currency of Iran.

<<< **IRATE** >>>

THE ADJECTIVE

Commonly seen clues: "Angry," "Furious," "Hopping mad," "Steaming," "Ticked off," and "Up in arms."

<<< **IRE** >>>

THE NOUN

As the noun form of "irate," commonly seen clues include "Anger," "Fury," "Infuriation," "Rage," and "Wrath." While the word will sometimes be clued as a verb meaning "to anger," this usage isn't very common in English today, and usually appears only in older unabridged dictionaries.

<<< **IRENE** >>>

THE GODDESS

Irene was the ancient Greek goddess of peace and one of the three Horae, the goddesses who controlled orderly life. Her Roman equivalent was Pax.

REAL PEOPLE

There's singer Cara, ballroom dancer Castle, actress Dunne, physicist Joliot-Curie, and actresses Pappas and Ryan.

IN FICTION

Irene is a major character in John Galsworthy's series of novels known as *The Forsyte Saga*. *Me, Myself & Irene* is a 2000 film in which Renée Zellweger portrays Irene. The 1919 Broadway musical *Irene*, revived in 1973 with Debbie Reynolds in the title role, is the source of the clue "Goodnight girl," because "Goodnight, Irene" appears in the lyrics of the title song.

--------- ◀◀◀ **IRIS** ▶▶▶ ---------

IN THE SKY

"Iris" is another word for "rainbow." This sense is derived from Iris, the ancient Greek goddess of the rainbow.

IN YOUR EYE

The iris is the part of the eye that gives it its color and is where the pupil is located.

THE FLOWER

The garden flower iris is known for its bearded blossoms. It is the state flower of Tennessee.

THE NAME

Iris Murdoch was an Irish novelist, who was portrayed in the 2001 film *Iris* by Judi Dench and Kate Winslet.

⟨⟨⟨ IRMA ⟩⟩⟩

THE NAME

The 1963 film *Irma la Douce* (literally "Irma the Gentle" in French) stars Shirley MacLaine in the title role. Irma Rombauer was the author of *The Joy of Cooking*. Irma Pince is the Hogwarts librarian in the Harry Potter book series. Irma is a waitress in the comic strip *Garfield*. The 1949 film *My Friend Irma* was the first screen pairing of Dean Martin and Jerry Lewis.

⟨⟨⟨ IRON ⟩⟩⟩

THE ELEMENT

Iron is often an ingredient in multivitamin pills. The ores from which iron is obtained include hematite, magnetite, and siderite. Iron is "pumped" by bodybuilders.

THE APPLIANCES

As a clothes-pressing tool, IRON will often be clued in verbal form, such as "Do a laundry job" and "Remove wrinkles." An iron is one of the playing pieces in the board game Monopoly. Branding irons are used by cowboys.

IN SPORTS

An iron is a type of golf club, used by players in the fairway.

THE ADJECTIVE

As an adjective, IRON is synonymous with "inflexible" or "unyielding."

————— <<< **IRS** >>> —————

THE ABBREVIATION

The IRS, or Internal Revenue Service, is the agency of the U.S. Treasury Department responsible for collecting taxes and enforcing tax laws. Clues for IRS refer to the aforementioned facts, as well as the tax form for individuals (Form 1040), the April 15 annual filing deadline for tax returns, and the audits and auditors associated with it.

————— <<< **ISA** >>> —————

BLANKETY-BLANKS

Colloquial quotes like "That __ lie!" and "This __ recording" can clue ISA, as well as the proverbs that end "is a penny earned" and "is a terrible thing to waste." Title clues include the songs "The Lady __ Tramp" and "Love __ Battlefield" and the novel and film, *The Heart __ Lonely Hunter*.

THE ABBREVIATION

"Isa." is short for the Old Testament book of Isaiah, which follows Song of Solomon and precedes Jeremiah.

Not So Fast!

"Parlor product": T A _

The answer can be TAN or TAT (short for "tattoo").

‹‹‹ ISEE ›››

THE ACKNOWLEDGMENT

Commonly seen clues are variations of "Ah, yes," "Phrase of understanding," and "That's clear."

‹‹‹ ISH ›››

THE SUFFIX

-ISH means "sort of," (similar to -ESQUE and -LIKE) and can be added to many words to form adjectives.

‹‹‹ ISLE ›››

IN GENERAL

Commonly seen nonspecific clues are variations of "Archipelago part" (an archipelago is a chain of islands), "Castaway's place," "Dot on a map," "Resort locale," and "Tropical spot."

SPECIFICALLY

Isles you're likely to encounter in crosswords include the major Hawaiian Islands (Hawaii, Kauai, Maui, and Oahu), England's Isle of Man and Isle of Wight, and the Italian isle of Capri.

‹‹‹ ITA ›››

BLANKETY-BLANKS

The colloquialisms "Call __ day," "Give __ go," "Give __ rest!," and "Give __ whirl" all clue IT A.

THE SUFFIX

-ITA is a diminutive feminine suffix in Spanish, most notably in the word *señorita*.

———— <<< **ITAL** >>> ————

THE ABBREVIATIONS

"Ital." may be short for "Italian" ("Romance lang.," "Milan's land: Abbr.," etc.), "Italy" ("Eur. country," "NATO member," "Switz. neighbor," etc.), or "italic" ("Emphatic type: Abbr.," "Slanted letters: Abbr.," etc.)

———— <<< **ITE** >>> ————

THE SUFFIX

-ITE is a suffix used for minerals (such as "magnetite"). It can also denote "citizen of" in words like "Israelite" and "urbanite," or denote a member of some political or other group (such as "laborite" and "socialite").

———— <<< **ITEM** >>> ————

THE NOUN

Commonly seen clues are variations of "Agenda listing," "Checkout-counter unit," and "Gossip-column tidbit."

———— <<< **ITO** >>> ————

BLANKETY-BLANKS

Colloquial quotes like "Am __ understand . . ." and "How was __ know?" can clue I TO.

THE NAME

Midori Ito is a former Japanese figure skater. Hirobumi Ito was a nineteenth-century Japanese prime minister. Los Angeles County Superior Court Judge Lance Ito presided over the 1995 O. J. Simpson murder trial.

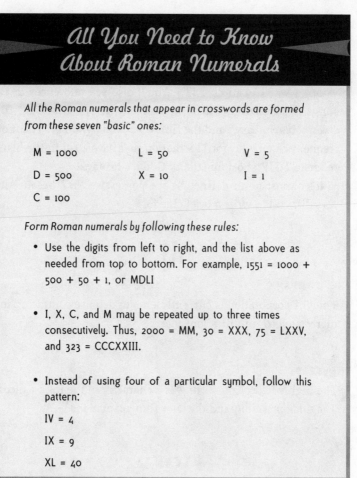

All You Need to Know About Roman Numerals

All the Roman numerals that appear in crosswords are formed from these seven "basic" ones:

M = 1000   L = 50   V = 5

D = 500   X = 10   I = 1

C = 100

Form Roman numerals by following these rules:

- Use the digits from left to right, and the list above as needed from top to bottom. For example, 1551 = 1000 + 500 + 50 + 1, or MDLI

- I, X, C, and M may be repeated up to three times consecutively. Thus, 2000 = MM, 30 = XXX, 75 = LXXV, and 323 = CCCXXIII.

- Instead of using four of a particular symbol, follow this pattern:

  IV = 4

  IX = 9

  XL = 40

<<< **ITON** >>>

BLANKETY-BLANKS

Colloquialisms like "Lay __ thick," "Pour __," "Take __ the chin," and "Try __ for size" can clue IT ON. Relevant song titles include "Blame It on the Bossa Nova" and "Let's Get It On."

───── <<< **ITS** >>> ─────

THE CONTRACTION

Colloquial quotes like "__ about time," "__ a deal!," and "For what __ worth" can clue ITS. You'll also see references to the songs "It's De-Lovely," "It's Impossible," "It's Not Unusual," "It's Over," "It's So Easy," and the film *It's a Wonderful Life*. The most frequent clue by far for ITS that doesn't have a fill-in-the-blank refers to TGIF, short for "thank God it's Friday."

It's almost never defined as the possessive "its," because it's very difficult to write a brief clue for.

───── <<< **ITT** >>> ─────

THE COMPANY

The ITT corporation is currently a major defense contractor, formerly a telecommunications giant.

THE BEAST

The highly hairy Cousin Itt was a character in the 1960s sitcom *The Addams Family* and the later film adaptations.

───── <<< **IVAN** >>> ─────

THE NAME

Ivan, the Russian equivalent of John, was the name of several Russian czars, most notably Ivan IV, whose nickname was "the Terrible." There's also financier Boesky, tennis pro Lendl, Nobel physiologist Pavlov, director Reitman, and author Turgenev. Ivan is one of the three title characters (the others are Dmitri and Alexei) in Dostoyevsky's *The Brothers Karamazov*.

Need to Know:
Crossword Spanish 101

The 25 Spanish words that appear most often as crossword answers (accent and diacritical marks, if any, are omitted):

amo (i love)

casa (house)

dos (two)

ella (she)

enero (January)

esta (is, this)

este (east)

mas (more)

nino (boy)

ole (shout of approval)

oro (gold)

otro (other, also *otra*)

rey (king)

rio (river)

sala (room)

senor (mister)

ser (to be)

sol (sun)

Sra. (Mrs.)

sur (south)

tia (aunt)

tio (uncle)

toro (bull)

tres (three)

uno (one, also *una*)

<<< **IVE** >>>

BLANKETY-BLANKS

Colloquial quotes like "__ been had!," "__ got it!," and "Now __ seen everything!" may clue IVE. You'll also see references to song titles like "I've Got a Crush on You," "I've Gotta Be Me," and "I've Got You Under My Skin," and the old TV game show *I've Got a Secret.*

THE SUFFIX

-IVE can be added to many words to form adjectives. A few of them are "combat," "distinct," "effect," and "secret."

————— <<< **IVES** >>> —————

THE NAME

The lithographers Nathaniel Currier and James Ives were partners in a famous nineteenth-century printmaking firm. Charles Ives was a modernistic composer of the early twentieth century, whose works include *Concord Sonata* and *The Unanswered Question.* Burl Ives was known both as a folk singer ("Blue Tail Fly" and "A Little Bitty Tear") and an actor (Big Daddy in the film *Cat on a Hot Tin Roof*).

LAOS. (*CENTRAL INTELLIGENCE AGENCY*)

the

LETTERS
K–L

———— ⟨⟨⟨ **KEN** ⟩⟩⟩ ————

THE NAME

There's PBS documentarian Burns, baseball star Griffey Jr., seventy-four-game *Jeopardy!* winner Jennings (a dedicated cross-word fan), novelist Kesey (*One Flew Over the Cuckoo's Nest*), actor Olin, and the doll that's the boyfriend of Barbie.

THE NOUN

In lowercase, "ken" is synonymous with "knowledge" or "understanding."

———— ⟨⟨⟨ **KNEE** ⟩⟩⟩ ————

THE JOINT

Commonly seen clues: "Baby bouncing spot," "Leg joint," "Pants part," and "Patella place."

———— ⟨⟨⟨ **LAD** ⟩⟩⟩ ————

THE KID

Commonly seen clues: "Little shaver," "Schoolboy," "Youngster," and "Youth."

———— ⟨⟨⟨ **LAIR** ⟩⟩⟩ ————

THE NOUN

A lair may be the den or resting place of a wild animal (such as a lion or a bear), or a person's secret retreat or hideout.

———— ⟨⟨⟨ **LANE** ⟩⟩⟩ ————

THE NOUN

A lane may be a narrow street, a highway division, a place to bowl, or a place to run a race.

THE NAME

In the *Superman* fictional universe, Lois Lane is a reporter for the *Daily Planet*, where she works with Clark Kent and Jimmy Olsen. She was portrayed most recently on film by Kate Bosworth in *Superman Returns*. Nathan Lane starred in the Broadway production of the Mel Brooks musical *The Producers*, and the 2005 film adaptation of the same name.

<<< **LAOS** >>>

THE COUNTRY

The southeast Asian nation of Laos is bordered by Cambodia, China, Myanmar, Thailand, and Vietnam. Its capital is Vientiane.

<<< **LAP** >>>

SITTING

Commonly seen clues in this sense: "Baby seat," "Santa's perch," and "Sitter's creation."

RACING

Athletic clues are similar to "NASCAR unit" and "Once around the track."

Not So Fast!

"Type of sandwich": _ _ R O

The answer can be the American HERO or the Greek GYRO.

THE VERB

To "lap up" is either to drink up or to receive enthusiastically.

———— <<< **LARA** >>> ————

THE NAME

Actress Lara Flynn Boyle was a regular on the TV series *The Practice*. Lara Croft is the heroine of the video game Tomb Raider, portrayed on film by Angelina Jolie. Lara is the name of the title character's beloved in the Boris Pasternak novel *Doctor Zhivago*, and is also the name of Superman's birth mother on the planet Krypton.

———— <<< **LARD** >>> ————

IN THE KITCHEN

Commonly seen clues in this sense: "Certain shortening," "Cooking fat," "Frying medium," and "Piecrust ingredient."

THE VERB

As a verb, "lard" means to "enrich," either with lard in the kitchen, or more figuratively, with evocative imagery in a literary work, for example.

———— <<< **LAS** >>> ————

THE SPANISH ARTICLE

"Las" is the Spanish feminine word for "the." City clue references include Las Cruces (in New Mexico), Las Palmas (in Spain's Canary Islands), and Las Vegas (in Nevada). The clue "Part of UNLV" refers to the University of Nevada at Las Vegas.

MUSICALLY SPEAKING

As the plural of the sixth note in a musical scale, las follow sols and precede tis. There's also "Singer's syllables" (as in "tra la la") and "'Deck the Halls' sounds" (as in "fa-la-la-la-la-la-la-la-la").

<<< **LATE** >>>

THE ADJECTIVE

Commonly seen clues: "After the deadline," "Not on time," "Past due," "Recent," and "Tardy."

<<< **LAVA** >>>

HOT STUFF

Commonly seen clues: "Molten rock," "Volcanic output," and references to well-known volcanoes such as Etna, Kilauea, Stromboli, and Vesuvius.

<<< **LAW** >>>

THE NOUN

Commonly seen clues: "Attorney's expertise," "Long-armed entity," "Order's partner," and "Statute." Noted lawyers that you'll see in clues include F. Lee Bailey, Johnnie Cochran, Alan Dershowitz, and the fictional Perry Mason.

THE NAME

The films of British actor Jude Law include the 2004 remake of *Alfie, Cold Mountain,* and the 2007 remake of *Sleuth.*

<<< **LEA** >>>

ON THE FARM

Commonly seen clues in the "pasture" sense: "Grassy area," "Grazing place," "Meadow," and "Rural expanse."

ON THE STAGE AND SCREEN

Actress Lea Thompson starred in the *Back to the Future* film series and the sitcom *Caroline in the City*. Lea Salonga won a Tony Award for her role in the Broadway musical *Miss Saigon*.

——— <<< **LEAN** >>> ———

THE ADJECTIVE

Commonly seen clues: "Lanky," "Like Jack Sprat's diet," "Low in fat," and "Skinny." The word can also mean "low in fat" as in "economical."

THE VERB

Commonly seen verb clues: "Be partial (to)," "Exert pressure (on)," and "Incline."

THE NAME

The films of British director Sir David Lean include *The Bridge on the River Kwai*, *Doctor Zhivago*, and *Lawrence of Arabia*.

——— <<< **LEASE** >>> ———

DON'T YOU BUY IT

Commonly seen noun clues: "Apartment document," "Kind of auto contract," and "Rental agreement." As a verb: "Charter," "Pay rent on," and "Take temporarily."

——— <<< **LED** >>> ———

THE VERB

Commonly seen verb clues: "Headed," "Set the pace," "Took charge of," and "Was in first place."

IN MUSIC

Led Zeppelin was a 1970s British rock band.

THE ABBREVIATION

Short for "light-emitting diodes," LEDs are used for the display on certain digital clocks and watches.

——————<<< **LEE** >>>——————

LAST-NAME REGULARS

The films of director Ang Lee include *Brokeback Mountain* and *Crouching Tiger, Hidden Dragon.* Ann Lee founded the American Shakers religious sect. Author Harper Lee wrote *To Kill a Mockingbird.* General Robert E. Lee commanded Confederate forces at the battles of Antietam, Fredericksburg, and Manassas (a.k.a. Bull Run), and surrendered to Grant at Appomattox Court House, Virginia. The films of director Spike Lee include *Crooklyn, Malcolm X,* and *Summer of Sam.*

LAST-NAME OCCASIONALS

Less frequently seen Lees include singer Brenda, entertainer Gypsy Rose, singer Peggy, and Spider-Man co-creator Stan.

FIRST NAME

There's actress Grant, former auto executive Iacocca, actors Majors and Marvin and actor/acting teacher Strasberg, and golfer Trevino.

MIDDLE NAME

There's attorney F. Lee Bailey, actor Tommy Lee Jones, rock singer Jerry Lee Lewis, and writer Edgar Lee Masters.

WITHOUT A CAPITAL

The lee side of a vessel or a mountain is the side that is sheltered or turned away from the wind.

--------- <<< **LEER** >>> ---------

THE NOUN/VERB

Commonly seen noun clues are variations of "Evil glance" and "Sly look." As a verb, there's "Eyeball," "Make eyes at," and "Ogle."

--------- <<< **LEG** >>> ---------

LITERAL

People and animals (especially chickens and turkeys, crossword-wise) have legs, as do chairs, tables, and trousers.

FIGURATIVE

A leg may be a part of a journey or a relay race, as well as either of the two nondiagonal sides of a right triangle.

--------- <<< **LEI** >>> ---------

IN HAWAII

Commonly seen clues are variations of "Luau neckwear," "Maui garland," "Oahu souvenir," and "Waikiki welcome."

Not So Fast!

"Piece of leather": S T R _ P

The answer can be STRAP or STROP.

‹‹‹ **LEN** ›››

THE NAME

There's sportscaster Berman, actor Cariou, pro football quarterback Dawson, and author Deighton.

‹‹‹ **LENA** ›››

THE NAME

Singer Lena Horne portrayed Glinda the good witch in the film version of *The Wiz*. Actress Lena Olin has appeared in such films as *Chocolat* and *Havana*.

ON THE MAP

Russia's Lena River flows through Siberia, including the city of Yakutsk.

‹‹‹ **LENO** ›››

THE NAME

Tonight Show host Jay Leno succeeded Johnny Carson in 1992 and will be succeeded by Conan O'Brien in 2009. His late-night TV rival is David Letterman. His autobiography is *Leading With My Chin*.

‹‹‹ **LENT** ›››

THE VERB

Commonly seen verb clues: "Advanced," "Allowed to use," "Gave for a while," and "Loaned."

ON THE CALENDAR

Pertaining to the Christian holiday, there's "Ash Wednesday begins it," "Easter preceder," "Mardi Gras follower," "Penitential period," "Spring season," and the wordplay clue "Fast time."

<<< LEO >>>

THE SIGN

The summer zodiac sign of Leo (the Lion) covers the period from July 23 through August 22. It follows Cancer and precedes Virgo. It is named for the constellation Leo, whose best known star is Regulus.

THE NAME

Famous Leos include author Buscaglia, baseball manager Durocher, and authors Rosten and Tolstoy. To date, thirteen popes have been named Leo. It is also the tabloids nickname for actor Leonardo DiCaprio.

<<< LES >>>

IN FRANCE

"*Les*" is a plural form of "the" in French, usually clued in crosswords as part of the title of the Victor Hugo novel *Les Misérables*, or the Broadway musical adaptation commonly known as *Les Miz*.

THE NAME

There's bandleader Brown, TV executive Moonves, and guitarist Paul.

<<< LESS >>>

THE ADVERB

Commonly seen clues: "Discounted by," "Marked down," "Minus," and "Not so much."

———— <<< **LET** >>> ————

THE VERB

Commonly seen verb clues: "Allow," "Charter," "Permit," and "Rent out." To "let down" is to disappoint, to "let off" is to pardon, and to "let up" is to ease. The clue "Admit" can be answered both by LET IN and LET ON (in two different senses of "admit").

THE NOUN

In tennis, a let is a play that is voided and must be redone.

———— <<< **LIAR** >>> ————

THE NOUN

Commonly seen clues: "Fibber," "Deceitful one," "Storyteller," and "Untrustworthy sort."

———— <<< **LID** >>> ————

LITERAL

A lid may be the cover of a container such as a jar or a coffee cup, a colloquial term for a hat, or a place for eye shadow. To "flip one's lid" is to be angry.

FIGURATIVE

A lid may also be the upper limit of something, such as a spending allowance.

———— <<< **LIE** >>> ————

THE UNTRUTH

Commonly seen noun clues in this sense: "False statement,"

"Fish story," "Prevarication," and "Whopper." As a verb: "Be deceitful," "Fudge facts," "Perjure oneself," and "Tell a fib."

OFF ONE'S FEET

Clues like "Recline" and "Sprawl" refer to the "relaxing" sense of LIE.

IN GOLF

On a golf fairway, a lie is the position of a ball.

‹‹‹ LIL ›››

THE CONTRACTION

As a short version of "little," there's rap artist Lil' Kim and comic-strip character Li'l Abner (resident of Dogpatch, created by Al Capp).

THE NAME

Diamond Lil was a 1928 Broadway play by Mae West, in which she portrayed the title role.

‹‹‹ LION ›››

THE BEAST

The "king of the jungle" wild feline is a summer sign of the zodiac (Leo) and the mascot of film studio MGM (also Leo). A group of lions is known as a "pride."

IN MYTH

In mythical multipart animals, a lion is a part of the griffin (part eagle also), the sphinx (part human also), the chimera (part goat and part serpent also), and manticore (part human and part dragon also). In Roman legend, the slave Androcles had a memorable encounter with a lion.

THE CHARACTERS

There's Simba in Disney's *The Lion King,* the Cowardly Lion in *The Wizard of Oz,* and Aslan in C. S. Lewis's *Chronicles of Narnia.* The Detroit Lions are an NFL team, and the athletic teams of Columbia University are known as the Lions.

FIGURATIVELY SPEAKING

A lion may also be a person of great importance and/or influence, such as a "literary lion."

<<< LIRA >>>

THE MONEY

The lira is the current monetary unit of Turkey, and was formerly the currency of Italy and Malta, both of which have been replaced by the euro.

<<< LOA >>>

THE SPEWER

Mauna Loa is an active volcano on the island of Hawaii. "Loa" is the Hawaiian word for "long"; "mauna" means "mountain."

<<< LON >>>

THE NAME

Lon Chaney and Lon Chaney Jr. were both actors remembered for their roles in horror films. There's also pro golfer Lon Hinkle and Lon Nol, who was prime minister of Cambodia from 1969–1972.

───◁◁◁ **LONI** ▷▷▷───

THE ONE AND ONLY

Actress Loni Anderson portrayed Jennifer on the sitcom *WKRP in Cincinnati* and was formerly married to actor Burt Reynolds.

───◁◁◁ **LORE** ▷▷▷───

THE NOUN

Commonly seen clues: "Folk wisdom," "Handed-down tales," "Oral history," and "Traditional knowledge."

───◁◁◁ **LOS** ▷▷▷───

IN SPAIN

Los is the Spanish masculine plural form of "the," the singular form being *el.*

IN THE U.S.

There are the cities of Los Angeles (as in "Part of UCLA") and Los Gatos in California, plus Los Alamos in New Mexico. Los Lobos is an American rock band.

───◁◁◁ **LOT** ▷▷▷───

THE NOUN

A lot may be a piece of real estate, a place to park a car or buy a car, a group of items up for auction, a large quantity of anything, or one's destiny. *Salem's Lot* is a Stephen King novel.

IN THE BIBLE

In the book of Genesis, Lot is the nephew of Abraham who escapes from the wicked city of Sodom.

⫷ **LOU** ⫸

THE NAME

There's comedian Costello (partner of Bud Abbott), CNN anchor Dobbs, baseball great Gehrig, football great Groza, and singer Rawls.

⫷ **LYE** ⫸

THE CHEMICAL

Lye is a strong solution of potassium hydroxide (a.k.a. "caustic potash") or sodium hydroxide, used to make soap, oven cleaners, and drain openers.

NEW YORK CITY'S METROPOLITAN MUSEUM OF ART
("THE MET," FOR SHORT), C. 1905. (LIBRARY OF CONGRESS)

the LETTER M

─── ‹‹‹ **MAC** ›››───

SLANGILY SPEAKING

As a slang term for a man, commonly seen clues include "Bub," "Buddy," "Fella," and "Pal." "Mac" is a colloquial term for the Apple Macintosh computer (alternative to the PC) and macaroni (as in "mac and cheese"), and a British slang term for a raincoat.

THE NAME

Bernie Mac was a comedic actor. Fleetwood Mac is a British rock band, active since the 1960s.

─── ‹‹‹ **MAE** ›››───

THE NAME

Mae Clarke, Mae West, and Mae Murray were all actresses. Rita Mae Brown is an author. Dr. Mae Jemison was the first African-American woman in space. Daisy Mae Yokum is the wife of the title character in the comic strip *Li'l Abner*.

THE PLANE

Winnie Mae was the airplane of aviator Wiley Post.

THE AGENCIES

"Mae" is part of the colloquial names of federal mortgage agencies, including Fannie Mae, Ginnie Mae, and Sallie Mae.

─── ‹‹‹ **MAMA** ›››───

ALL IN THE FAMILY

Commonly seen clues are usually variations of "Cry from a crib" and "Papa's partner." There's also the Mama Bear from the

Goldilocks story, 1960s pop singer Mama Cass Elliot, and the 1980s sitcom *Mama's Family*, in which Vicki Lawrence portrayed Mama.

———— <<< **MAO** >>> ————

THE LEADER

Mao Tse-tung (a.k.a. Mao Zedong) was the Communist leader of the People's Republic of China from 1949 into the 1970s. Chairman Mao's "Red Book" of quotations was carried by the Chinese during his tenure. As a revolutionary figure in the 1930s, he led the "Long March" retreat of his followers. Mao instituted the "Great Leap Forward" economic plan in 1958. The "Cultural Revolution" was a 1960s power struggle within the Chinese Communist Party; Mao's civilian supporters in this struggle were called the Red Guard. In 1972, President Nixon met with Mao in China.

———— <<< **MAP** >>> ————

GEOGRAPHICALLY SPEAKING

Commonly seen clues: "Atlas page," "Glove compartment item," "Navigator's need," and "Road guide."

———— <<< **MAR** >>> ————

THE VERB

Commonly seen verb clues: "Damage," "Scratch up," "Spoil," and "Tarnish."

THE ABBREVIATION

As a short form of the month of March, there's "Apr. preceder," "Feb. follower," "St. Patrick's Day mo.," and "When spr. starts."

—————— <<< **MATA** >>> ——————

THE SPY

The Dutch-born Mata Hari was an infamous spy during World War I. She was portrayed by Greta Garbo in a 1932 film.

—————— <<< **MEAT** >>> ——————

LITERALLY

Commonly seen edible clues include "Butcher's wares," "Ham or lamb," "Potatoes' partner," and "What vegans won't eat." The edible portion of a nut is called the "meat."

FIGURATIVELY

"Meat" can also mean the essential point of something, clued by "Crux," "Essence," "Gist," and "Nitty-gritty."

—————— <<< **MEET** >>> ——————

THE VERB

Commonly seen clues: "Comply with" (as a demand), "Convene," "Encounter," and "Run into."

THE NOUN

In this sense, a meet is an athletic contest, usually of track-and-field or swimming events.

—————— <<< **MEL** >>> ——————

THE NAME

There's cartoon voicemaster Blanc, football great Blount, director Brooks, actors Ferrer and Gibson, baseball great Ott, and singers Tillis and Tormé.

Not So Fast!

"Flower part": _ E _ A L

The answer can be PETAL or SEPAL.

<<< **MEN** >>>

THE GUYS

Commonly seen clues: "Blokes," "Fellows," "Fraternity members," and "Gents."

THE TOKENS

Men may also be the playing pieces used in board games, particularly checkers and chess.

<<< **MENU** >>>

AT THE RESTAURANT

Commonly seen clues in this sense: "Bill of fare," "Course listing," "Restaurant reading," and "Waiter's handout."

ELSEWHERE

A menu can also be a list of items to choose from in other venues, particularly on a computer screen.

<<< **MER** >>>

IN PARIS

"Mer" is the French word for "sea." *La Mer* is an orchestral work by French composer Claude Debussy. *Mal de mer* is the French idiom for "seasickness."

————— ‹‹‹ **MERE** ››› —————

THE ADJECTIVE

Commonly seen clues: "Insignificant," "Nothing but," "Paltry," and "Simple."

IN PARIS

"Mère" is the French word for "mother," which you'll see as a clue now and then.

————— ‹‹‹ **MESA** ››› —————

ON THE MAP

A mesa is a small plateau or tableland (similar to a butte), having steep walls and a relatively flat top, common in the Southwest. The city of Mesa, Arizona, is near Phoenix. Colorado's Mesa Verde National Park has ruins of prehistoric cliff dwellings.

————— ‹‹‹ **MESS** ››› —————

THE DISORDER

Commonly seen clues in this sense: "Disarray," "Hodgepodge," "Pigsty," and "Predicament."

TO THE TROOPS

"Mess" is a military term for a meal taken as a group, in a mess hall.

————— ‹‹‹ **MET** ››› —————

THE VERB

As the past tense of "meet," there's "Encountered," "Greeted," "Happened upon," and "Ran into."

IN THE BIG APPLE

The New York Mets are a National League baseball team, whose home games were played in Shea Stadium from 1962 to 2008, and the newly built Citi Field from 2009. "The Met" is a colloquial term for both New York City's Metropolitan Opera House, part of the Lincoln Center complex, and the Big Apple's Metropolitan Museum of Art.

<<< **METE** >>>

THE VERB

Commonly seen clues: "Allot," "Dole (out)," "Distribute," and "Parcel (out)."

<<< **MIA** >>>

THE NAME

Actress Mia Farrow (daughter of actress Maureen O'Sullivan) had the title role in the film *Rosemary's Baby* and was Hannah in the Woody Allen film *Hannah and Her Sisters*. She was once married to singer Frank Sinatra. Mia Hamm is a former star for the U.S. women's national soccer team. Uma Thurman portrays a character named Mia in the film *Pulp Fiction*.

IN ROME

"*Mia*" is the Italian feminine pronoun for "my." "*Mamma mia!*" is an Italian exclamation, *Mamma Mia!* is a musical play based on the songs of the Swedish pop group Abba, adapted into the 2008 film of the same name.

<<< **MOE** >>>

THE NAME

Moe Howard was the leader of the Three Stooges comedy team,

whose other members included Larry Fine and Curly Howard. American skier Tommy Moe won a gold medal at the 1994 Winter Olympics. There are two notable cartoon Moes: the bartender on the sitcom *The Simpsons*, and the bully in the comic strip *Calvin and Hobbes*.

─────── <<< **MORE** >>> ───────

THE ADJECTIVE

Commonly seen clues: "Additional," "Encore!," "Extra," and "Oliver Twist's request" (from the Dickens novel).

THE SURNAME

British author Sir Thomas More, author of *Utopia*, is the subject of the play and film *A Man for All Seasons*.

SCOTLAND'S URQUHART CASTLE, OVERLOOKING LOCH NESS. (*FOTOLIA.COM*)

the

LETTER

N

<<< **NAB** >>>

THE VERB

Commonly seen clues: "Arrest," "Catch red-handed," "Collar," and "Run in."

<<< **NANA** >>>

IN THE FAMILY

As a term for "grandmother," commonly seen clues include: "Babysitter, at times," "Family nickname," and "Mom's mom."

IN LITERATURE

Nana is a novel by French author Émile Zola. Nana is the pet dog of the Darling family in James Barrie's *Peter Pan*.

<<< **NAP** >>>

THE TIME-OUT

Commonly seen clues in this sense: "Afternoon break," "Catch some z's," "Forty winks," "Short snooze," and "Siesta."

THE FUZZ

Nap is also the short fuzzy ends of fibers on the surface of fleece and fabric products such as flannel, towels, and carpets.

<<< **NARC** >>>

THE COP

A narc is a police officer that enforces drug laws, such as agents of the DEA (Drug Enforcement Administration).

<<< **NASA** >>>

UP IN THE AIR

Clues about the National Aeronautics and Space Administration are most likely to refer either to its spacecraft (such as space shuttles *Atlantis, Columbia, Discovery,* and *Endeavour*), its space projects (such as Mercury, Gemini, and Apollo), or its best-known astronauts (such as Neil Armstrong, Buzz Aldrin, and John Glenn).

<<< NAT >>>

THE NAME

There's jazz cornetist Adderley (brother of "Cannonball"), singer Nat "King" Cole (father of singer Natalie), and nineteenth-century slave-rebellion leader Turner.

IN SPORTS

A member of the National League's Washington (D.C.) Nationals team may be called a "Nat" for short.

<<< NATO >>>

THE WESTERN DEFENSE FORCE

Founded in 1949, the North Atlantic Treaty Organization is headquartered in Brussels, Belgium. The Warsaw Pact was its former counterpart among European Communist states.

Not So Fast!

"Type of flower": _ A _ SY

The answer can be DAISY, PANSY, or TANSY.

<<< NBA >>>

IN SPORTS

The National Basketball Association is usually clued either generically (such as "Cagers' grp.," "Court org.," or "Hoops grp.") or in reference to one of its teams (such as the Bucks, Bulls, Cavs, Hornets, Lakers, Magic, Mavs, Rockets, and Wizards).

<<< NEA >>>

THE UNION

The National Educational Association is a labor union that represents public school teachers.

THE AGENCY

The National Endowment for the Arts is a federal agency that funds artistic projects and public TV (PBS), for example.

<<< NEAR >>>

THE ADJECTIVE

Commonly seen adjective clues: "At hand," "Close by," "Imminent," and "Not far."

THE VERB

Commonly seen verb clues: "Approach," "Get close to," and "Move toward."

<<< NEAT >>>

THE ADJECTIVE

As a synonym for "orderly," there's "All in place," "Clean-cut,"

"Tidy," and "Uncluttered." Meaning "without ice" (as a drink), there's "Bar order," "Straight up," and "Undiluted."

THE EXCLAMATION

As a word of approval, commonly seen clues include "Cool!," "Nifty!," and "Swell!."

───────── <<< **NED** >>> ─────────

REAL

There's actor Beatty, composer Rorem, and Australian outlaw Kelly (sort of the Australian Jesse James).

FICTIONAL

Ned Flanders is the neighbor of the title family in the animated sitcom *The Simpsons*. *Waking Ned Devine* is a 1998 film. Ned Nickerson is the boyfriend of teenage sleuth Nancy Drew.

───────── <<< **NEE** >>> ─────────

FROM PARIS

"Née," the French word for "born," is often seen on society pages and bridal notices before a woman's maiden name, as in "Jane Smith, *née* Jones."

───────── <<< **NEED** >>> ─────────

THE VERB

Commonly seen verb clues: "Can't do without," "Call for," "Must have," and "Require."

THE NOUN

As a noun, there's "Necessity," "Requirement," "Scholarship criterion," and "Something essential."

⟨⟨⟨ **NEER** ⟩⟩⟩

THE CONTRACTION

"Ne'er" is a poetic form of the adverb "never." A ne'er-do-well is a good-for-nothing individual.

⟨⟨⟨ **NEMO** ⟩⟩⟩

THE NAME

Nemo is the captain of the submarine *Nautilus* in the Jules Verne novel *Twenty Thousand Leagues Under the Sea*. *Finding Nemo* is an animated film of 2003, whose title character is a clownfish.

⟨⟨⟨ **NEO** ⟩⟩⟩

THE PREFIX

Meaning "new" or "recent," "neo" can be added in front of words such as "classical," "colonial," and "natal." The prefix "paleo-" (meaning "ancient") is the opposite of "neo-."

IN THE MOVIES

In the 1999 film *The Matrix*, Keanu Reeves has the lead role of Neo.

⟨⟨⟨ **NEON** ⟩⟩⟩

THE GAS

The inert (a.k.a. "noble") gas neon is commonly used in advertising signs.

ON THE ROAD

The Dodge Neon is a formerly produced model of compact car.

───── <<< **NERD** >>> ─────

THE NOUN

Commonly seen clues: "Dweeb," "Geek," "Social outcast," and "Uncool one."

───── <<< **NERO** >>> ─────

LONG AGO

The infamous Roman emperor Nero, nephew of Caligula and husband of Octavia, was the successor of Claudius and the predecessor of Galba. Nero is portrayed by Peter Ustinov in the 1951 film *Quo Vadis*.

OF LATE

Franco Nero is an Italian actor, and Peter Nero is a pianist and conductor. Nero Wolfe is a fictional detective created by author Rex Stout.

───── <<< **NESS** >>> ─────

THE NAME

Federal agent Eliot Ness, adversary of Chicago gangster Al Capone, led the group of Prohibition agents known as "The Untouchables." He was portrayed in the 1960s TV series *The Untouchables* by Robert Stack and in the 1987 film of the same name by Kevin Costner.

THE LAKE

Scotland's Loch Ness is the reputed home of a giant creature known as the Loch Ness monster.

IN LOWERCASE

A ness is a point of land that projects into the sea or other body of water. Clues in that sense are "Cape," "Headland," and "Promontory."

———— <<< **NEST** >>> ————

THE RESIDENCE

A nest may be a home for insects (such as hornets) or birds, as well as a snug retreat for people.

Need to Know: The Greek Alphabet

It will be very useful for you to know all 24 letters in the Greek alphabet, in order. Not only do most of these appear frequently in crosswords, but the letters that precede and follow them are often used as clues, such as "Sigma preceder" for RHO. With the shortest answers in standard crosswords being three letters, the two-letter ones appear only as plurals.

Alpha	Eta	Nu	Tau
Beta	Theta	Xi	Upsilon
Gamma	Iota	Omicron	Phi
Delta	Kappa	Pi	Chi
Epsilon	Lambda	Rho	Psi
Zeta	Mu	Sigma	Omega

THE VERB

In addition to the verb form of the sense above, items that fit together or within each other, such as Russian dolls, are said to "nest."

<<< **NET** >>>

MONEYWISE

Commonly seen clues in this sense: "After taxes," "Bottom-line," "End up with," and "Profit."

THE FABRIC

Nets are used by fishermen and lepidopterists (butterfly collectors), as a circus safety device, and in the sports of badminton, tennis, and volleyball.

IN CYBERSPACE

As a short form of "Internet," you may see clues like "Something to surf." The Internet suffix ".net" is a common one for Web sites.

<<< **NEV** >>>

ON THE MAP

As an abbreviation for Nevada, it'll be worth your while to know the state's nickname ("The Silver State"), neighbors (Arizona, California, Idaho, Oregon, and Utah), and major cities (Carson City, Las Vegas, Reno, and Sparks).

<<< **NICE** >>>

THE ADJECTIVE

Commonly seen adjective clues include "Agreeable," "Genial," "Kindly," and "Pleasant."

THE ENCOURAGING WORD

"Good job!" and "Well done!" clue NICE in an exclamatory sense.

ON THE MAP

The European resort city of Nice is on the French Riviera.

———— <<< **NIL** >>> ————

THE UN-QUANTITY

Commonly seen clues: "Goose egg," "Nothing," "Zero," and "Zilch."

———— <<< **NILE** >>> ————

ON THE MAP

One of the world's longest rivers, the Nile flows through the African nations of Egypt, Sudan, Uganda, Tanzania, and Rwanda, and the cities of Aswan, Cairo, Khartoum, and Luxor. Cleopatra sailed her royal barge in the Nile. Lake Victoria is part of the Nile's source. *Death on the Nile* is a novel by Agatha Christie.

THE COLOR

Nile is a shade of bluish green.

Not So Fast!

"Aria, for one": S O _ _

The answer can be SOLO or SONG.

‹‹‹ **NINE** ›››

THE COUNT

There are nine innings in a standard baseball game, nine defensive players on a baseball field, nine Muses in mythology, and nine Supreme Court justices. There are nine holes each on the "front nine" and "back nine" halves of a golf course.

THE NUMBER

Nine is the largest digit, the square of the number three, the emergency CB radio channel, and the lowest card in pinochle.

THE TIME

"Midmorning" or "Midevening" may define NINE a.m. or p.m. The latter time is an hour for prime-time network TV broadcasts.

‹‹‹ **NNE** ›››•

THE ABBREVIATION

NNE stands for the direction of north-northeast, which is the point opposite south-southwest (SSW) on a compass. You'll often see city clues like "Dayton-to-Toledo dir.," where the second city is located north-northeast of the first. NNE and all the other compass points can be seen in weather reports (referring to wind direction) and on the screens of GPS devices.

‹‹‹ **NOEL** ›››

THE NOUN

"Noel" may refer to a Christmas carol or the yuletide season.

THE NAME

Sir Noël Coward was an actor, composer, and playwright.

<<< **NOLTE** >>>

THE NAME

The films of actor Nick Nolte include *Affliction, Cape Fear, 48 HRS., Lorenzo's Oil,* and *The Prince of Tides.*

<<< **NONE** >>>

THE UN-QUANTITY

In addition to many of the same clues that can define NIL ("Goose egg," "Nothing," "Zilch," etc.), there's "All's opposite," "Bar __ (without exception)," and "__ of the above."

<<< **NOON** >>>

ON THE CLOCK

Commonly seen clues: " 'High' time," "Lunch time for many," "Midday," and "When shadows are shortest."

<<< **NOR** >>>

THE CONJUNCTION

Commonly seen clues include "Common correlative," "Likewise not," "Negative connector," and "Neither's partner." Fill-in-the-blanks: "Hide __ hair," "Neither fish __ fowl," and "Neither here __ there."

THE ABBREVIATION

As a short version of "Norway," there's "NATO member," "Neighbor of Swed.," and "Scand. nation."

<<< **NORA** >>>

REAL

Nora Dunn was once a regular on the TV series *Saturday Night*

Live. Nora Ephron is a movie director and screenwriter. Nora Roberts is a romance novelist.

FICTIONAL

Nick and Nora Charles are the sleuth spouses in the Dashiell Hammett novel *The Thin Man* and own Asta the terrier; Myrna Loy portrayed Nora in the 1930s film series based on the novel. Nora Helmer is a character in the Ibsen play *A Doll's House.*

‹‹‹ NOS ›››

THE PLURAL

Commonly seen clues in this sense: "Denials," "Negative votes," "Refusals," and "Turndowns."

THE ABBREVIATION

As a short version of "numbers," there's "CPA's expertise," "Figs.," "Lottery choices: Abbr.," and "Phone bk. listings."

‹‹‹ NOSE ›››

LITERALLY SPEAKING

Commonly seen clues: "Facial feature," "Scent sensor," "Sniffer," and "Smeller." Owners of famous noses include Cyrano de Bergerac, Jimmy Durante, Pinocchio, and flying reindeer Rudolph. Airplanes and rocket ships also have noses.

FIGURATIVELY SPEAKING

The "nose" of a wine is its aroma. As a verb, "nose" is synonymous with "snoop." To "nose out" is to defeat by a narrow margin.

———— <<< **NOT** >>> ————

THE EXCLAMATION

The 1992 film *Wayne's World* popularized the use of NOT at the end of a sentence to indicate what has just been stated isn't true. Clues like "Hardly!" and "Only kidding!" refer to this sense.

BLANKETY-BLANKS

"__ a chance!," "I should say __!," "__ on your life!," and "__ to worry!" may also clue NOT.

THE ADVERB

NOT is only occasionally clued as to how it's most used in English, such as "Negative word," "Ten Commandments word," and "Word of denial."

———— <<< **NOTE** >>> ————

THE MISSIVE

As a short letter, there's "Brief message" and "Memo."

THE VERB

Commonly seen verb clues include "Jot down" and "Observe."

OTHER NOUNS

A note can also be a piece of paper currency, an IOU, or a musical tone.

———— <<< **NOVA** >>> ————

IN THE SKY

A nova is a type of star whose brightness increases suddenly, then gradually fades.

ON THE TUBE
Nova is a TV science series seen on PBS.

ON THE MAP
Nova Scotia is an eastern province of Canada. Nova Scotia lox ("Nova" for short) is a variety of smoked salmon.

ON THE ROAD
The Nova was a model of Chevrolet automobile manufactured from 1962–1979 and again from 1985–1988.

———— <<< **NRA** >>> ————

THE OLD AGENCY
The NRA, short for National Recovery Administration, was created in 1933, early in the first term of President Franklin Roosevelt, as part of his New Deal program. Its logo was a blue eagle.

TODAY
The National Rifle Association is a gun-advocacy group headed at one time by actor Charlton Heston. It publishes *American Hunter* magazine. Commonly seen clues in this sense include "Influential D.C. lobby," "Marksman's org.," and "Second Amendment supporter: Abbr."

OKRA. (FOTOLIA.COM)

the
LETTER
O

---<<< **OAF** >>>---

THE NOUN

Commonly seen clues: "Buffoon," "Clumsy one," "Lummox," and "Stumblebum."

---<<< **OAHU** >>>---

ON THE MAP

Oahu, the second largest of the Hawaiian Islands, is the home of Honolulu, Pearl Harbor, the volcanic peak Diamond Head, and Waikiki Beach. Nearby islands include Kauai and Molokai. The TV series *Hawaii Five-O*, *Lost*, and *Magnum, P.I.* have been filmed there.

---<<< **OAR** >>>---

THE IMPLEMENT

As a type of paddle, commonly seen clues include "Boathouse gear," "Dinghy implement," "Galley tool," and "Rower's need." An oar may also be a person who rows, especially as a member of a sculling or crew team. As a verb, to "oar" is to propel a vessel with oars.

Not So Fast!

"Chilly": C O _ _

The answer can be COOL or COLD.

—— ‹‹‹ **OAS** ››› ——

THE ALLIANCE

Founded in 1948, the Organization of American States comprises all the independent countries of the Western Hemisphere.

—— ‹‹‹ **OAT** ››› ——

THE EDIBLE

Commonly seen clues: "Bran source," "Cereal grain," "Feedbag morsel," and "Granola ingredient."

—— ‹‹‹ **OBI** ››› ——

IN JAPAN

An obi is a broad sash worn as a belt with a kimono.

IN THE MOVIES

In the *Star Wars* film series, Obi-Wan Kenobi is a good-guy Jedi Knight. He is portrayed by Sir Alec Guinness in the original trilogy and by Ewan McGregor in the prequel trilogy.

—— ‹‹‹ **OBIE** ››› ——

FOR THE SHOW

Obie Awards are presented by New York City's *Village Voice* newspaper for off-Broadway productions.

—— ‹‹‹ **OBOE** ››› ——

IN THE ORCHESTRA

The oboe is a double-reed woodwind instrument. Its woodwind "cousins" in the orchestra are the bassoon, clarinet, and flute.

Types of oboes include the English horn and heckelphone. In Serge Prokofiev's *Peter and the Wolf,* an oboe plays the part of the duck.

◀◀◀ **OCALA** ▶▶▶

ON THE MAP

The Florida city of Ocala, seat of Marion County, is located between Gainesville and Orlando.

◀◀◀ **OCEAN** ▶▶▶

ON THE GLOBE

The world's oceans are the Antarctic, Arctic, Atlantic, Indian, and Pacific. The ocean is the realm of the mythical gods Poseidon and Neptune. Generic clues include: "Bounding main," "Liner's locale," and "Where the buoys are."

FIGURATIVELY SPEAKING

An ocean can also be a vast expanse or a large quantity of anything.

◀◀◀ **ODD** ▶▶▶

UNEXPECTED

Commonly seen clues in this sense: "Eerie," "Peculiar," "Uncanny," and "Unusual."

UNMATCHED

In this sense, there's "Lacking a mate," "Left over," and "Unpaired."

UN-EVEN

An odd number (such as 37 or 101) is one that is not evenly divisible by two. A bet on all the odd numbers is often made in roulette.

———— <<< **ODE** >>> ————

THE POEM

An ode is a lyric poem often written to praise something or someone. Noted writers of odes include Samuel Taylor Coleridge, Thomas Gray, John Keats, Percy Bysshe Shelley, William Wordsworth, the ancient Roman poet Horace, and the ancient Greek poet Pindar.

———— <<< **ODIE** >>> ————

IN THE COMICS

Odie is the dimwitted dog in the comic strip *Garfield*.

———— <<< **ODIN** >>> ————

IN MYTH

Odin was the chief of the Aesir race of gods in Norse mythology, the husband of Frigg, and the father of Thor. His hall is Valhalla, which is located in the land of Asgard. He rode an eight-legged horse named Sleipnir.

———— <<< **ODOR** >>> ————

WHAT THE NOSE KNOWS

Synonymous clues include "Aroma," "Bouquet," "Fragrance," and "Scent." More descriptive clues: "Air freshener target," "Fish market feature," and "Skunk's weapon."

◂◂◂ OER ▸▸▸

IN VERSE

"O'er" is the poetic form of the preposition "over," the opposite of "neath." The two best-known occurrences of the word are in "The Star-Spangled Banner" ("O'er the ramparts we watched . . .") and "Jingle Bells" ("O'er the fields we go").

◂◂◂ OGLE ▸▸▸

THE VERB

Commonly seen clues: "Eye boldly," "Gawk at," "Look like a wolf," and "Stare at."

◂◂◂ OGRE ▸▸▸

THE MENACE

Commonly seen generic clues: "Cruel one," "Dictatorial boss," "Folklore villain," and "Meanie." The title character of the *Shrek* animated film series (voiced by Mike Myers) is an ogre.

◂◂◂ OHARA ▸▸▸

REAL

Author John O'Hara wrote *Pal Joey* and *Butterfield 8*. Actress Maureen O'Hara's films include *Rio Grande*, *The Quiet Man*, and the original version of *The Parent Trap*.

FICTIONAL

Scarlett O'Hara is the heroine of the Margaret Mitchell novel *Gone With the Wind*, in which she marries Rhett Butler. Her Atlanta estate is called Tara. Actress Vivien Leigh won an Academy Award for portraying her in the film version.

<<< **OHARE** >>>

THE HUB

Named for a World War II aviator, Chicago's O'Hare is one of the world's busiest airports.

<<< **OHIO** >>>

THE BUCKEYE STATE

Clues for Ohio the state usually refer either to its major cities (Akron, Canton, Cincinnati, Cleveland, Columbus, Dayton, and Toledo), its neighboring states (Indiana, Kentucky, Michigan, Pennsylvania, and West Virginia) or its universities (Kent State and Oberlin). Seven U.S. presidents were born in Ohio, second only to Virginia.

THE RIVER

The Ohio River is formed at Pittsburgh from the Allegheny and Monongahela rivers. Other cities on the Ohio include Cincinnati, Louisville, and Wheeling.

<<< **OHO** >>>

THE SHOUT

Very similar in meaning to AHA, commonly seen clues include "Eureka!," "I see!," "So that's it!," and "Sound of surprise."

<<< **OIL** >>>

IN AUTOS

There's "Black gold," "Friction reducer," "OPEC product," and "Texas tea."

IN ART

Many famous paintings are oils, such as Van Gogh's *Starry Night*.

IN FOOD

Oil goes with vinegar in salad dressings. Sources of edible oil include corn, olives, peanuts, sesame, and sunflowers.

⟨⟨⟨ OKRA ⟩⟩⟩

THE VEGGIE

The pod vegetable is popular in Creole cookery, where it is an ingredient of gumbo.

⟨⟨⟨ OKS ⟩⟩⟩

THE VERB

Commonly seen verb clues: "Authorizes," "Endorses," "Greenlights," and "Signs off on."

THE NOUN

Noun clues: "Agreements," "Approvals," and "Go-aheads."

⟨⟨⟨ OLA ⟩⟩⟩

THE SUFFIX

The slangy suffix -OLA can be added to words such as "pay," "plug," "scram," and "schnozz."

⟨⟨⟨ OLAF/OLAV ⟩⟩⟩

THE NAME

The two spellings of the Norwegian male name are seen about

equally often in crosswords. It's the name of Norway's patron saint (Minnesota has a St. Olaf College), and has been the name of five Norwegian kings.

<<< OLD >>>

THE ADJECTIVE

Commonly seen clues: "Ancient," "Antique," "Outdated," and "Stale."

<<< OLE >>>

THE CHEER

Olé is a Spanish shout of approval, frequently heard at a bullfight (a.k.a. corrida).

THE MUSIC SHOW

Nashville's weekly *Grand Ole Opry*, which debuted in 1925, is America's oldest regular radio program.

<<< OLEG >>>

THE NAME

Almost all clues for OLEG refer to Russian-born fashion designer Cassini.

<<< OLEO >>>

THE EDIBLE

Commonly seen clues include "Bread spread," "Butter alternative," "Margarine," and "Muffin topping."

<<< OLGA >>>

THE NAME

Most clues for OLGA refer to Russian gymnast Korbut, medal winner at the 1972 and 1976 Summer Olympics. Olga is also one of the title characters in the Anton Chekhov play *Three Sisters*, and a character in the Tchaikovsky opera *Eugene Onegin*.

<<< OLIO >>>

THE MISCELLANY

Commonly seen clues: "Hodgepodge," "Mixed bag," "Potpourri," and "This and that."

<<< OLIVE >>>

THE FRUIT

Olives may be found in an antipasto or a Greek salad, and in martinis, sometimes with a pimiento inside. Named for the fruit is the color olive green.

THE TOON

The lanky Olive Oyl is the girlfriend of Popeye the Sailor.

<<< OLLA >>>

IN SPAIN

An olla is a Spanish stewpot or earthenware jar. "Olla podrida" (literally "rotten pot") is a spicy Spanish stew.

<<< OMAHA >>>

IN THE U.S.

Omaha, on the Missouri River, is the largest city in Nebraska.

The annual College World Series is played there, and Boys Town is nearby. Celebrities born there include actors Fred Astaire and Marlon Brando and 1970s U.S. president Gerald Ford.

ACROSS THE SEA
Omaha Beach was the code name for one of the landing sites of the D-Day Normandy invasion during World War II.

─────── <<< **OMAN** >>> ───────

ON THE MAP
The Mideast nation of Oman is located on the Arabian peninsula, on the Arabian Sea, Persian Gulf, and the Gulf of Oman. Its capital is Muscat, and its neighbors are Saudi Arabia, the United Arab Emirates, and Yemen.

─────── <<< **OMAR** >>> ───────

THE NAME
There's World War II general Bradley, actor Epps, Persian poet Khayyám (a.k.a. "the Tentmaker," author of *The Rubáiyát*), actor Sharif, and baseball player Vizquel.

Not So Fast!

"Leslie Caron film": _ I _ I

The answer can be GIGI or LILI.

◀◀◀ **OMEN** ▶▶▶

THE NOUN

Commonly seen clues: "Augury," "Harbinger," "Portent," "Seer's sighting," and "Sign of the future."

◀◀◀ **OMIT** ▶▶▶

THE VERB

Commonly seen clues: "Exclude," "Leave out," "Pass over," and "Skip."

◀◀◀ **OMNI** ▶▶▶

THE PREFIX

Meaning "all," OMNI- can be added to words such as "bus," "potent," and "present."

THE NAME

Omni Hotels is an upscale lodging chain. *Omni* was a science magazine, the Omni was an Atlanta sports arena, and the Dodge Omni automobile was manufactured from 1978–1990.

◀◀◀ **ONA** ▶▶▶

BLANKETY-BLANKS

Colloquialisms "__ lark," "Not __ bet," "__ shoestring," "Stop __ dime," "Three __ match," and "__ trial basis" all clue ON A. Relevant film titles include *Cat on a Hot Tin Roof*, *On a Clear Day You Can See Forever*, *Snakes on a Plane*, and *Strangers on a Train*. Song titles include "Come on-a My House," "Leaving on a Jet Plane," and "Put on a Happy Face."

<<< **ONCE** >>>

THE ADVERB/NOUN

Commonly seen clues: "A single time," "Fairy tale starter" (as in "Once upon a time"), "Formerly," and "Years ago."

<<< **ONE** >>>

THE ADJECTIVE

Clock clues are variations of "Early afternoon" and "Wee hour." Non-numerical clues include "Indivisible," "Like-minded," "Undivided," and "United." Numerical clues include "Best-seller's position," "Binary digit," "It's next to nothing," and "Low number."

THE MONEY

Commonly seen cash clues: "Buck," "Four quarters," "Single," and "Small bill."

THE PRONOUN

There's "A person," "Neuter pronoun," and "Nonspecific individual."

<<< **ONEA** >>>

THE RATING

1-A was the highest draft rating issued by the Selective Service System, indicating that a person was eligible for unrestricted military service.

<<< **ONEAL** >>>

THE SURNAME

There's actor Ryan (of the film *Love Story*), basketball star Shaquille, and actress Tatum (Ryan's daughter, who won an Oscar for *Paper Moon*).

<<< **ONIT** >>>

BLANKETY-BLANKS

The colloquial clues "Don't bet __!," "Put a lid __," and "Step __ (hurry)" all clue ON IT.

THE PHRASE

Clues like "Doing the job" and "Taking action" are sometimes seen also.

<<< **ONO** >>>

THE NAME

Yoko Ono, widow of ex-Beatle John Lennon, performed with him on the album *Double Fantasy*. The 1970s Plastic Ono Band consisted of Ono, Lennon, and other rock-music notables. Lennon adopted Ono as his middle name.

<<< **ONOR** >>>

BLANKETY-BLANKS

"__ about," "__ after," "__ before," and "__ close to schedule" are about the only ways to clue ON OR.

<<< **ONSET** >>>

THE NOUN

Commonly seen clues: "Beginning," "Get-go," "Inception," "Square one," and "Start."

─── <<< ONT >>> ───

ON THE MAP

As an abbreviation for the Canadian province of Ontario, ONT can be clued by its neighboring states (Michigan, Minnesota, New York), neighbouring provinces (Manitoba and Quebec), and cities (such as Hamilton, Ottawa, Toronto, and Windsor).

─── <<< ONTO >>> ───

THE PREPOSITION

Commonly seen prepositional clues are variations of "Aware of" and "Not fooled by."

BLANKETY-BLANKS

Clued as two words, there's "Catch __," "Hang __," and "Latch __."

─── <<< ONUS >>> ───

THE NOUN

The three most frequent clues are "Burden," "Obligation," and "Responsibility."

─── <<< OONA >>> ───

THE NAME

Lady Oona Chaplin was the wife of film legend Charlie Chaplin. Her father was playwright Eugene O'Neill; her best-known child is actress Geraldine.

◂◂◂ OOZE ▸▸▸

THE VERB

Commonly seen verb clues: "Flow slowly," "Move like molasses," "Seep," and "Trickle."

THE NOUN

The occasional noun clues are similar to "Gooey stuff" and "Slimy substance."

◂◂◂ OPAL ▸▸▸

THE GEM

The opal is a milky-white iridescent gemstone, the birthstone for October. Mexico is a source of the "fire opal," though most of the world's opals come from Australia.

◂◂◂ OPEC ▸▸▸

THE OIL CARTEL

The members of the Vienna-based Organization of the Petroleum Exporting Countries include Ecuador, Iraq, Qatar, and Venezuela.

◂◂◂ OPEN ▸▸▸

THE ADJECTIVE

Commonly seen adjective clues: "Amenable," "Candid," "Ready for business," and "Store sign."

THE VERB

Commonly seen verb clues: "Dentist's request," "Start the bidding," and "Unlock."

THE NOUN

An open is a type of tournament (such as in golf or tennis) in which professionals and amateurs may compete.

<<< **OPERA** >>>

IN MUSIC

OPERA is usually defined either by well-known operas (such as *Carmen, Il Trovatore, La Bohème, La Traviata, The Magic Flute, Otello, Porgy and Bess,* and *Tosca*), operatic composers (such as Bizet, Mozart, Puccini, Verdi, and Wagner), or opera venues (such as the Met at New York City's Lincoln Center and Milan's La Scala).

<<< **OPIE** >>>

THE KID

A very young Ronny Howard (who later became an eminent director known as Ron) portrayed Opie Taylor, son of Mayberry sheriff Andy Taylor, in the 1960s sitcom *The Andy Griffith Show.* Opie's great-aunt was named Bee (short for Beatrice).

THE ARTIST

Once in a while, a clue will refer to British portrait painter John Opie.

<<< **OPT** >>>

THE VERB

Commonly seen clues include "Be decisive," "Get off the fence," and "Make a choice." To "opt for" is to choose, to "opt out" is to decline to participate.

Not So Fast!

"Praise highly": E X _ _ _

The answer can be EXALT or the nearly synonymous EXTOL.

<<< ORA >>>

BLANKETY-BLANKS

"Are you a man __ mouse?" or "Feast __ famine" most often clue OR A.

AS ONE WORD

"Ora" is an anatomical term for "mouths." *"Ora"* is the Latin word for "pray"; *Ora pro nobis* means "pray for us."

<<< ORAL >>>

THE ADJECTIVE

Commonly seen adjective clues: "Spoken," "Verbal," and "Vocal." People and things that may be oral include history, hygiene, surgeons, thermometers, traditions, and vaccines.

THE NOUN

An oral (short for "oral examination") is often a requirement for a graduate school degree.

THE NAME

Tulsa's Oral Roberts University is named for the television evangelist.

⟨⟨⟨ ORATE ⟩⟩⟩

THE VERB

Commonly seen clues: "Declaim," "Get on a soapbox," "Give a speech," "Make an address," and "Speak at length."

⟨⟨⟨ ORB ⟩⟩⟩

THE SHAPE

An orb can be a sphere, a globe, an eye, or a heavenly body. An orb atop a scepter is a symbol of royalty.

⟨⟨⟨ ORCA ⟩⟩⟩

THE FISH

Also known as the killer whale, the black-and-white orca is the largest member of the dolphin family. SeaWorld performer Shamu is an orca, as is the title character of the 1993 film *Free Willy*. In the film *Jaws*, *Orca* is the boat captained by Robert Shaw's character.

⟨⟨⟨ ORE ⟩⟩⟩

THE ROCK

Ores are metal-bearing rocks or minerals that are often mined. Commonly seen related clues include "Assay material," "Lode load," "Prospector's find," and "Refinery input." Types of ores include bauxite (aluminum), galena (lead), and hematite (iron).

THE ABBREVIATION

"Ore." is an abbreviation for Oregon, usually defined in this sense in terms of its neighbors (California, Idaho, Nevada, and

Washington), cities (Eugene, Salem), or Mount Hood, its tallest peak.

—————— <<< **OREL** >>> ——————

THE NAME

Orel Hershiser is a former big-league pitcher.

ON THE MAP

Located on the Oka River, the Russian city of Orel was the birthplace of writer Ivan Turgenev.

—————— <<< **OREO** >>> ——————

THE MUNCHIE

About a half-trillion of Nabisco's cream-filled sandwich cookies have been sold since they were introduced in 1912. Double Stuf Oreos have more cream filling than the regulars. Oreos are often an ingredient in Cookies and Cream ice cream.

—————— <<< **ORO** >>> ——————

IN SPAIN

"Oro" is the Spanish word for "gold." *Oro y plata* ("gold and silver") is the state motto of Montana.

—————— <<< **ORR** >>> ——————

ON THE ICE

Hockey Hall of Famer Bobby Orr played most of his career with the Boston Bruins, and was a multiple winner of the NHL's Art Ross Trophy, Conn Smythe Trophy, Hart Trophy, and Norris Trophy.

---<<< **ORSO** >>>---

NOT EXACTLY

Commonly seen clues: "About," "Approximately," "Roughly," and "Thereabouts."

---<<< **OSCAR** >>>---

THE PEOPLE

Famous Oscars include designer de la Renta, lyricist Hammerstein, pianist Levant, hot-dog merchant Mayer, pianist Peterson, basketball great Robertson, writer Wilde, and the grouchy *Sesame Street* muppet. Oscar Madison is the sloppy roommate of neatnik Felix Unger in Neil Simon's *The Odd Couple*.

THE TROPHY

The Academy Award statuette weighs a little over eight pounds.

---<<< **OSLO** >>>---

ON THE MAP

The Scandinavian city of Oslo (formerly known as Christiania) is the capital of Norway. The annual Nobel Peace Prize is awarded there, and the 1952 Winter Olympics were held there.

---<<< **OSS** >>>---

THE ABBREVIATION

The Office of Strategic Services, a World War II spy agency, was the predecessor of the CIA.

‹‹‹ **OTT** ›››

ON THE DIAMOND

Baseball Hall of Famer Mel Ott played his entire career with the New York Giants.

‹‹‹ **OTTER** ›››

IN THE WATER

Otters are web-footed aquatic mammals known for their playful behavior. Their relatives in the weasel family include the beaver, mink, and skunk.

‹‹‹ **OTTO** ›››

FICTIONAL

In the comic strip *Beetle Bailey*, Otto is the pet bulldog of Sergeant Snorkel. The school-bus driver in the animated sitcom *The Simpsons* is also named Otto.

REAL

Otto von Bismarck was a nineteenth-century German chancellor. Otto Klemperer was an orchestra conductor. Otto Preminger was a movie director.

‹‹‹ **OUR** ›››

THE PRONOUN

Commonly seen clues include "Not their," "Sharer's word," and "Your and my." "Our" is the first word of the Lord's Prayer. Titles with the word include the soap opera *Days of Our Lives*, the 1950s sitcom *Our Miss Brooks*, and the Thornton Wilder play *Our Town*.

Our Gang, a.k.a. *The Little Rascals,* is the umbrella title of a series of short children's films of the 1930s, rerun endlessly on TV for the past fifty years.

<<< **OVA** >>>

THE PLURAL

"Ova" is the Latin word for "eggs." In English, it's the scientific term for egg cells.

<<< **OVEN** >>>

THE HOT SPOT

There are microwave ovens, toaster ovens, Dutch ovens, and rotisserie ovens. Other types of ovens include the kiln (for pottery), oast (for hops or malt), and tandoor (in Indian cookery). Bakeries and pizzerias are the two types of establishments with ovens that are most often cited in clues.

<<< **OVER** >>>

THE PREPOSITION

Commonly seen prepositional clues: "Above," "Beyond," "More than," and "Throughout."

THE ADJECTIVE

Commonly seen adjective clues are variations of "Done" and "Ended."

THE INTERJECTION

"Over" is often used in radio communications to indicate that the speaker has finished and is waiting for a reply.

◀◀◀ **OWE** ▶▶▶

THE VERB

Commonly seen clues: "Be indebted to," "Be in the red," "Carry a balance," and "Have obligations."

◀◀◀ **OXEN** ▶▶▶

THE BOVINES

Commonly seen clues: "Beasts of burden," "Farm animals," "Plow pullers," and "Yoked pair."

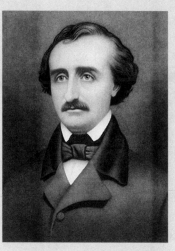

PORTRAIT OF EDGAR ALLAN POE,
C. 1896, BY WILLIAM SARTAIN.
(*LIBRARY OF CONGRESS*)

the
LETTER
P

◀◀◀ PAAR ▶▶▶

THE GOOD LISTENER

Jack Paar (pronounced "par") was the host of NBC's *Tonight Show* from 1957 to 1962, succeeding Steve Allen and succeeded by Johnny Carson.

◀◀◀ PAD ▶▶▶

THE NOUN

Computers have mouse pads, NASA has launching pads, ponds have lily pads, beds have mattress pads, stenographers have writing pads, and hippies live in pads.

THE VERB

In slang, to "pad" something is to unnecessarily expand or add to it, as a speech or an expense account.

◀◀◀ PAL ▶▶▶

THE NOUN

Commonly seen clues: "Buddy," "Chum," "Crony," and "Sidekick."

◀◀◀ PALE ▶▶▶

THE ADJECTIVE

Though it's also a verb and a noun, PALE is almost always clued as an adjective, such as "Ashen," "Like some ales," "White as a sheet," and "Wan."

<<< PAN >>>

THE COOKWARE

Skillets and woks are types of pans, often partnered with pots. Pizzas, dessert pies, and turkeys may be baked in pans.

IN THE PAPER

To "pan" a film is to give it a bad review. As a noun, it's the review itself.

THE NAME

Pan was the ancient Greek pipe-playing god of pastures and forests.

<<< PAPA >>>

THE PATRIARCH

Commonly seen generic clues are "Dad" and "Family man." The Papa Bear was one of the three bears encountered by Goldilocks. "Papa" was the nickname of composer Joseph Haydn and author Ernest Hemingway. The song "Papa Loves Mambo" was popularized by Perry Como, "Papa Don't Preach" by Madonna.

Not So Fast!

"Modify": _ M E N D

The answer can be AMEND or the similar EMEND.

────── <<< PAR >>> ──────

ON THE COURSE

Par is the standard score for a hole, one lower than a bogey and one higher than a birdie. Par for an entire 18-hole golf course is usually around 72.

OFF THE COURSE

Commonly seen generic clues: "Average," "Norm," and "Standard."

────── <<< PASSE >>> ──────

THE ADJECTIVE

Commonly seen clues: "No longer in style," "Obsolete," "Old hat," and "Outdated."

────── <<< PAT >>> ──────

LOWERCASE

A pat may be a portion of butter or an encouraging touch. As an adjective/adverb, it means "exactly."

UPPERCASE

Famous Pats include singer Benatar, TV commentator Buchanan, game-show host Sajak, and 1970s First Lady Nixon.

────── <<< PEA >>> ──────

THE LEGUME

Peas are ingredients in stews, split-pea soup, and potpies. Their color is "pea green." "The Princess and the Pea" is a fairy tale by Hans Christian Andersen.

<<< **PEER** >>>

THE NOUN

A peer may be a social equal (as a member of a jury) or a British noble (such as earl or duke).

Need to Know: Greek Goddesses

The Greek goddesses that appear most often in crosswords (with Roman equivalents in parentheses):

APHRODITE (VENUS): goddess of beauty, daughter of Zeus, mother of Ares

ARTEMIS (DIANA): goddess of the hunt, daughter of Zeus, twin sister of Apollo

ATHENA (MINERVA): goddess of wisdom, daughter of Zeus

DEMETER (CERES): goddess of agriculture, sister of Zeus and Hera

EOS (AURORA): goddess of the dawn, sister of Selene

ERIS: goddess of discord

HERA (JUNO): queen of the gods, sister and wife of Zeus

HESTIA (VESTA): goddess of the hearth, sister of Zeus and Hades

IRENE (PAX): goddess of peace, daughter of Zeus

IRIS: goddess of the rainbow

RHEA (OPS): mother of the gods, mother of Zeus, Hera, and Hades

SELENE (LUNA): goddess of the moon, sister of Eos

THE VERB

To "peer at" something is to look at it narrowly and/or searchingly.

———— <<< **PELE** >>> ————

THE NAME

Pélé is the nickname of Brazilian soccer star Edson Arantes do Nascimento, who was an active player from the 1950s to the 1970s.

———— <<< **PEN** >>> ————

FULL OF INK

You should know these manufacturers of pens: Bic, Cross, Mont Blanc, Paper Mate, and Parker. Clues like "Sword beater" refer to the old proverb, "the pen is mightier than the sword." As a verb, to "pen" means to write or compose something.

FULL OF OINK

Other domesticated animals besides pigs may be kept in pens, such as horses and sheep.

IN THE CLINK

As a slang term for "prison," there's "Cooler," "Pokey," and "Slammer."

IN THE AIR

"Pen" is the term for a female swan.

———— <<< **PER** >>> ————

THE PREPOSITION

Commonly seen clues: "According to," "Apiece," "Each," and the slangy synonym "A pop." It is the "p" in the abbreviations mph (miles per hour) and rpm (revolutions per minute). In phrases from the Latin, "per capita" means "per person" and "per diem" means "per day."

<<< **PESO** >>>

THE MONEY

The peso is the monetary unit of Argentina, Chile, Colombia, Cuba, the Dominican Republic, Mexico, the Philippines, and Uruguay. Crossword clues will often refer to cities in these countries, such as "Cancún cash."

<<< **PEST** >>>

THE NOUN

Commonly seen clues: "Annoyance," "Nudnik," "Nuisance," and "Pain in the neck."

<<< **PETE** >>>

THE NAME

Famous Petes include jazz clarinetist Fountain, Rose of baseball, tennis pro Sampras, folk singer Seeger, and the dog (a.k.a. Petey) in the *Little Rascals* (a.k.a. *Our Gang*) series of kids' short films.

<<< **PLEA** >>>

THE NOUN

In court, a plea might be "guilty," "not guilty," "nolo contendere" (not contending the charge), or may be the result of plea bargaining. Generic clues include "Appeal," "Entreaty," and "Request."

———— <<< **POE** >>> ————

THE WRITER

You'll want to know these works written by Edgar Allan Poe: "Annabel Lee," "The Bells," "The Black Cat," "The Gold Bug," "The Purloined Letter," "The Raven," "The Tell-Tale Heart," and "Ulalume."

———— <<< **PRE** >>> ————

THE PREFIX

PRE- can be added in front of umpteen words, such as "historic," "mature," and "school." It is similar in meaning to the prefix "ante-" and the opposite of "post-."

ON THE MAP

Grand-Pré (French for "Great Meadow"), Nova Scotia, is the site of a Canadian national park and is the setting for the Henry Wadsworth Longfellow poem "Evangeline."

———— <<< **PRO** >>> ————

THE NOUN

As the short form of "professional," commonly seen clues include "Expert," "Golf teacher," "Money player," and "Veteran."

THE ADVERB

As a synonym for "in favor of," there's "Debate side," "Favoring," "For," and "Supporting."

———— <<< **PSI** >>> ————

THE LETTER

Psi is the twenty-third of twenty-four letters in the Greek alphabet, preceded by chi and followed by omega. Both an uppercase and lowercase psi (Ψ,ψ) resemble a trident or pitchfork.

THE ABBREVIATION

"Psi" stands for "pounds per square inch," which is a measure of the pressure of things such as auto tires.

THE UNEXPLAINED

"Psi" is a term for any psychic phenomenon, such as ESP.

⟨⟨⟨ **PSST** ⟩⟩⟩

THE SOUND

Commonly seen clues are all variations of "Attention getter," "Hey, you!," and "Subtle signal."

⟨⟨⟨ **PTA** ⟩⟩⟩

THE ABBREVIATION

As a short form of Parent-Teacher Association, commonly seen clues are usually variations of "Bake sale sponsor" and "Grade school org." "Harper Valley P.T.A." is a country-music song of 1968.

TWO MEN STANDING BESIDE A REO SPEED WAGON TRUCK, WHICH
BROUGHT ESKIMO PIES TO PRESIDENT HARDING AT THE
WHITE HOUSE, 1922. (*LIBRARY OF CONGRESS*)

the
LETTER
R

‹‹‹ RAE ›››

THE NAME

There's actress Rae Dawn Chong, comic actress Charlotte Rae, soul singer Corinne Bailey Rae, Scottish explorer John Rae, and the 1979 film *Norma Rae*, for which Sally Field won an Oscar in the title role.

‹‹‹ RAF ›››

THE ABBREVIATION

The Royal Air Force is the British equivalent of the U.S. Air Force. During World War II, the RAF successfully defended the British skies against Germany, which prompted the famous quote from British prime minister Winston Churchill, "Never . . . was so much owed by so many to so few."

‹‹‹ RAGE ›››

THE PASSION

As a noun, there's "Anger," "Frenzy," and "Fury." As a verb: "Blow up," "Fly off the handle," and "Go ballistic."

THE FASHION

A rage may also be something very popular or in fashion, often for just a short time.

‹‹‹ RAH ›››

THE EXCLAMATION

Commonly seen clues: "Cheer syllable," "Encouraging word," "Go, team!," and "Stadium shout."

———<<< **RAIN** >>>———

THE WEATHER

Commonly seen noun clues: "Desert rarity," "Drought relief," "Picnic spoiler," and "Wet forecast." As a verb, there's "Come down," "Pour," "Precipitate," and "Shower."

———<<< **RAISE** >>>———

THE NOUN

Commonly seen noun clues: "Poker ploy," "Salary increase," "Union demand," and "Worker's reward."

THE VERB

As a verb, there's "Boost," "Bring up," "Elevate," and "Lift."

———<<< **RAM** >>>———

THE BEAST

Generic clues that refer to the male sheep include: "Ewe's mate," "Flock animal," and "Woolly male." The ram Aries is a spring sign of the zodiac. The Dodge Ram, named for the beast, is a model of pickup truck. The St. Louis Rams is an NFL team. The athletic teams of Fordham University are known as the Rams.

THE WEAPON

Noun clues in this sense: "Battering device" and "Door buster." As a verb, there's "Bash," "Butt into," and "Hit broadside."

HIGH-TECH

RAM stands for "random access memory," an important part of computers.

─────── <<< **RAN** >>> ───────

THE VERB

In the speedy sense, there's "Jogged," "Raced," and "Took off." In the managerial sense, there's "Headed," "Managed," and "Operated." In the political sense, there's "Sought office" and "Was on the ticket."

─────── <<< **RANI** >>> ───────

THE ROYAL

In India, a rani (also spelled "ranee") is the wife of a rajah, or a reigning queen, or a princess.

─────── <<< **RANT** >>> ───────

THE VERB

Commonly seen verb clues: "Carry on," "Go ballistic," and "Talk wildly."

THE NOUN

In the noun sense, there's "Angry speech," "Bluster," and "Tirade."

Not So Fast!

"Prohibit": B A _

The answer can be BAR or BAN.

───<<< **RARE** >>>───

THE ADJECTIVE

In the "uncommon" sense, there's "Exceptional," "Hard to find," "Infrequent," and "Seldom seen." In the culinary sense, there's "Opposite of well done," "Pink in the center," and "Steakhouse order."

───<<< **RASP** >>>───

THE TOOL

A rasp is a coarse file that is used mainly on wood. The related verb means "scrape" or "grate."

THE SOUND

People who are hoarse speak with a rasp.

───<<< **RAT** >>>───

THE PERSON

Commonly seen "human" clues include "Snitch," "Scoundrel," "Tattletale," and "Turncoat." As a verb, there's "Spill the beans" and "Squeal."

THE BEAST

"Four-legged" clues include: "Lab animal," "Mouse relative," and "Pied Piper follower."

───<<< **RATA** >>>───

BLANKETY-BLANKS

"Pro rata" means "proportionally." "Rat-a-tat" is a knocking or rapping sound.

⟨⟨⟨ **RATE** ⟩⟩⟩

THE VERB

Commonly seen verb clues: "Appraise," "Assess," "Evaluate," "Have status," and "Size up."

THE NOUN

As a noun, there's "Bank posting," "Fixed charge," "Pace," and "Tempo."

⟨⟨⟨ **RBI** ⟩⟩⟩

ON THE DIAMOND

In baseball, RBI is short for "run batted in." Clues are variations on "Slugger's stat."

⟨⟨⟨ **RCA** ⟩⟩⟩

THE BRAND

The RCA brand of consumer electronics is often defined in terms of its competitors, which include Philips, Sharp, Sony, Toshiba, and Zenith. RCA's mascot is a dog named Nipper.

⟨⟨⟨ **REA** ⟩⟩⟩

THE ACTOR

The films of Irish actor Stephen Rea include *The Crying Game*, *Michael Collins*, and *V for Vendetta*.

THE AGENCY

The New Deal–era Rural Electrification Administration was created in 1935 to provide electric power to rural areas.

————<<< **READ** >>>————

THE VERB

Commonly seen present-tense clues: "Interpret," "Leaf through," "Peruse," and "Pore over."

INSIDER'S TIP: Keep in mind that the past tense of "read" is also "read," though pronounced differently.

————<<< **REAL** >>>————

THE ADJECTIVE

Commonly seen clues: "Actual," "Authentic," "Bona fide," "Genuine," and "Sincere."

————<<< **REAP** >>>————

THE VERB

In the agricultural sense, there's "Bring in the sheaves," "Collect, as crops," "Harvest," and "Use a scythe." In the figurative sense, there's "Earn, as profits" and "Realize."

————<<< **REAR** >>>————

THE VERB

Commonly seen verb clues: "Bring up," "Elevate," and "Nurture."

THE NOUN

In a general sense, there's "Back" and "Tail end." In the "sitting" sense, there's "Caboose," "Posterior," "Rump," etc.

‹‹‹ REB ›››

AT WAR

A reb (short for "rebel") was a Confederate soldier during the Civil War, often under the command of General Robert E. Lee. Wearing a gray uniform, he was the adversary of a Yank.

‹‹‹ REBA ›››

THE NAME

Country singer Reba McEntire was the star of the sitcom *Reba*, which aired from 2001 to 2007.

‹‹‹ RED ›››

THE COLOR

Red things referred to in crossword clues include checkers, cherries, rubies, stop signs, traffic lights, and wines. Shades of red include carmine, crimson, and scarlet. Red is a sign of embarrassment or sunburn; red ink symbolizes a loss in business.

‹‹‹ REDO ›››

THE VERB

Commonly seen clues: "Decorate anew," "Fix up," "Make over," and "Overhaul."

‹‹‹ REED ›››

IN MUSIC

A reed is a part of various musical instruments, such as the clarinet, oboe, and saxophone, which are part of the "reed instrument" family.

THE PLANT

A reed is also the tall stalk of certain types of grass that typically grow in marshy areas.

<<< REEL >>>

THE NOUN

A reel may hold fishing line (accompanying a rod), or hold movie film in a projection booth. A reel is also a type of dance, specifically the country dance also known as the Virginia reel.

THE VERB

Commonly seen verb clues: "Stagger," "Walk unsteadily," and "Whirl."

<<< REESE >>>

THE NAME

There's singer/actress Della Reese, baseball Hall of Famer Pee Wee Reese, and actress Reese Witherspoon, plus the candy maker of Reese's Pieces fame.

<<< REF >>>

IN SPORTS

Refs (short for "referees") are officials in boxing, football, hockey, and tennis. Football refs are called "zebras," for the black-and-white striped shirts they wear.

<<< REIN >>>

THE NOUN

Commonly seen noun clues: "Bridle attachment," "Harness part," "Horse stopper," and "Jockey's brake."

Not So Fast!

"Ripped off": T O _ _

In the literal sense, the answer can be TORE or TORN; in the slang sense, it can also be TOOK.

THE VERB

As a verb, there's "Check," "Hold back," and "Restrain."

<<< **REL** >>>

THE ABBREVIATION

Clues as a short form for "relative" are variations of "Fam. member" and "Kin: Abbr." Cluing "religion," there's "Faith: Abbr.," "Prot. or Cath.," and "Seminary subj."

<<< **REM** >>>

AT NIGHT

REM, short for "rapid eye movement," is a stage of sleep during which dreams occur.

IN MUSIC

R.E.M. is an American rock band, whose best-known tunes include "Losing My Religion" and "The One I Love."

IN SCIENCE

In physics, a rem is a unit of radiation.

◀◀◀ RENE ▶▶▶

THE FIRST NAME

There's philosopher Descartes, tennis pro Lacoste, artist Magritte, and actress Russo.

◀◀◀ RENO ▶▶▶

THE CITY

Reno, Nevada, located near Lake Tahoe on the Truckee River, is the seat of Washoe County. It's nicknamed "The Biggest Little City in the World" and is home to numerous gambling casinos.

THE NAME

Janet Reno served as Bill Clinton's attorney general, succeeding William Barr and preceding John Ashcroft.

◀◀◀ RENT ▶▶▶

FOR TENANTS

Commonly seen noun clues in this sense: "Apartment payment," "Budget expense," "Housing cost," and "Monopoly payment" (as in the board game). Verb clues: "Charter," "Lease," and "Pay for the use of."

THE OTHER VERB

"Rent" is also the past tense of "rend," meaning to split or tear.

THE SHOW

The Broadway show *Rent*, based on the opera *La Bohème*, won the Best Musical Tony Award for 1996.

—————<<< **REO** >>>—————

THE CAR

The Reo Motor Car Company made cars and trucks from 1904 to the 1970s. Its name was derived from the initials of founder Ransom Eli Olds, who started up Oldsmobile before Reo.

THE ROCK GROUP

Founded in the late 1960s and still active, rock band REO Speedwagon took its name from a truck model of the Reo Motor Car Company. The group has had two #1 Billboard tunes, "Keep on Loving You" and "Can't Fight This Feeling."

—————<<< **REP** >>>—————

THE PEOPLE

As a short form of (a generic) "representative," there's "Account exec," "Agent, for short," and "Salesperson." Short for "representative" (as in a member of Congress), there's "D.C. VIP" and "One of 435." Short for "Republican," there's "Dem. rival" and "GOP member."

THE THINGS

Short for "reputation," there's "One's good name" and "Public image." Short for "repetition" (used especially in exercise), there's "Gym unit," "Iron-pumping unit," and "Workout unit."

—————<<< **RES** >>>—————

AT THE BAR

"Res" is a term in law for a legal matter.

AT THE PIANO

Res are the second notes of a musical scale, following dos and preceding mis.

AT THE COMPUTER

"Res" is short for "resolution," as in a "hi-res monitor."

AT HOME

"Res." is an abbreviation for "residence."

————— <<< **RESET** >>> —————

THE VERB

Commonly seen verb clues include "Adjust, as a clock," "Put back to zero," and references to various devices that have a reset button, such as bowling alleys, furnaces, pedometers, and stop-watches.

————— <<< **REST** >>> —————

THE BREAK

As a verb, there's "Kick back," "Relax," "Take five," and "Unwind." As a noun: "Breather" and "Time off." On a piece of music, a rest is a marking that indicates an interval of silence between notes.

WHAT'S LEFT

In this sense, there's "Balance," "Others," and "Remainder."

————— <<< **RET** >>> —————

THE ABBREVIATION

As a short form of "retired," commonly seen clues include

"Emeritus: Abbr.," "No longer working: Abbr.," "On a pension: Abbr.," and "Part of AARP" (American Association of Retired Persons).

<<< **RHO** >>>

THE LETTER
Rho is the seventeenth letter of the Greek alphabet, coming after pi and before sigma.

<<< **RIATA** >>>

A riata (a.k.a. lasso and lariat) is a rope used by cowboys, South American gauchos, and rodeo riders. Note that the word can also be spelled "reata," but that spelling appears in crosswords far less often.

<<< **RID** >>>

THE VERB
Commonly seen clues: "Clear (of)," "Disencumber," "Free (of)," and "Purge." Note that the past tense of "rid" is also "rid."

<<< **RILE** >>>

THE VERB
Commonly seen clues: "Agitate," "Rub the wrong way," "Tee off," "Tick off," and "Vex."

<<< **RIN** >>>

BLANKETY-BLANKS
The German shepherd Rin Tin Tin was one of Hollywood's biggest stars of the silent-film era. The phrase "Oysters 'R' in sea-

son" refers to the old adage that oysters should be eaten only during months whose names have the letter "r."

‹‹‹ **RIO** ›››

IN SPANISH AND PORTUGUESE

"Rio" is the Spanish and Portuguese word for "river."

IN SOUTH AMERICA

Rio de Janeiro is the former capital of Brazil. "Rio" for short, it's a popular cruise port and site of an annual Carnival festival just before Lent. Rio is the home of Sugar Loaf Mountain, and Copacabana and Ipanema beaches.

IN NORTH AMERICA

The Rio Grande forms the border between Texas and Mexico, and flows through New Mexico and Colorado.

IN THE MOVIES

Blame It on Rio is a Michael Caine film. *Rio Bravo* and *Rio Lobo* are John Wayne films. *Road to Rio* is a Bob Hope/Bing Crosby film, one of their famous "Road" movies.

IN THE GARAGE

Rio is a model of Kia automobile.

‹‹‹ **RIOT** ›››

THE NOUN

In the "disorder" sense, there's "Mob scene," "Public disturbance," and "Uproar." In the humorous sense, there's "Barrel of laughs," "Hilarious one," and "Knee-slapper."

THE VERB

Commonly seen verb clues are similar to "Go hog wild" and "Run amok."

―――――――――<<< **RIPE** >>>―――――――

THE ADJECTIVE

Commonly seen clues: "Mature," "Pickable," and "Ready for harvest."

―――――――――<<< **RISE** >>>―――――――

THE VERB

Commonly seen verb clues: "Ascend," "Get out of bed," "Go up," and "Stand."

THE NOUN

As a noun, there's "Ascent," "Slope," and "Upswing."

―――――――――<<< **RITA** >>>―――――――

THE NAME

There's singer Coolidge, author Rita Mae Brown, actresses Hayworth and Moreno, comic Rudner, and the meter maid in a Beatles song.

―――――――――<<< **RITE** >>>―――――――

THE NOUN

A rite is a solemn ceremony, often of a religious nature. Rites mentioned in crossword clues: baptism, bar mitzvah, communion, confirmation, and marriage.

<<< **RNA** >>>

THAT'S LIFE

Common clues such as "Genetic material" and "Substance in cells" can define DNA as well as RNA. "Protein messenger" and "Retrovirus material" are unique to RNA.

<<< **RNS** >>>

THE ABBREVIATIONS

As a short form for "registered nurses," there's "ER workers," "Hosp. employees," "ICU staffers," and "IV monitors."

<<< **ROAD** >>>

THE PATHWAY

Commonly seen clues: "Highway," "Line on a map," "Thoroughfare," and "Way to go."

<<< **ROB** >>>

THE VERB

Commonly seen verb clues: "Hold up," "Rip off," "Steal from," and "Stick up."

THE NAME

The two best-known Robs are actor Lowe and director Reiner.

<<< **ROD** >>>

THE NOUN

Things with rods include curtains, fishing gear, nuclear reactors, and the retina of the eye, which has groups of rodlike cells called "rods."

THE NAME

There's tennis pro Laver, sci-fi writer and TV host Serling, and singer Stewart.

<<< **ROE** >>>

IN THE SEA

Roe is fish eggs, certain types of which are used for caviar.

IN THE WOODS

A roe is also a type of small deer.

IN THE COURT

The names Richard Roe and Jane Roe are often used for anonymous parties in court proceedings, such as in the landmark Supreme Court decision *Roe v. Wade.*

<<< **ROI** >>>

IN PARIS

"*Roi*" is the French word for "king." Clues may refer to specific French kings such as Louis XIV, the dauphin (the eldest son of a French king), or "*palais,*" the French word for "palace."

Not So Fast!

"Something funny": _ _ O T

The answer can be RIOT or HOOT.

———<<< **ROLE** >>>———

THE NOUN

Commonly seen generic clues include "Auditioner's goal," "Casting slot," "Function," and "Part to play." You'll also see references to numerous specific roles in well-known works, and roles played by specific well-known performers.

———<<< **RON** >>>———

THE NAME

There's Tarzan portrayer Ely, director Howard, presidential son Reagan, and Ron Weasley, friend of Harry Potter in the J. K. Rowling novels.

———<<< **RONA** >>>———

THE NAME

Gossip reporter Barrett and author Jaffe are the two best-known Ronas.

———<<< **ROSE** >>>———

THE FLOWER

There's "American Beauty, for example," "Thorny bloom," and "Valentine's Day gift."

THE DRINK

Rosé is a variety of pink wine.

THE VERB

As the past tense of "rise," there's "Ascended" and "Got up."

THE NAME

Rose Kennedy was the mother of JFK, Betty White portrayed Rose Nylund on the sitcom *The Golden Girls*, and Pete Rose is a retired baseball player.

<<< **ROT** >>>

THE VERB

Commonly seen verb clues: "Deteriorate," "Go bad," and "Spoil."

THE NOUN

Any synonym for "nonsense" may be seen in this sense, such as "Baloney," "Claptrap," "Hogwash," and "Malarkey."

<<< **ROTE** >>>

THE NOUN

Commonly seen clues: "Dull routine," "Learning method," and "Repetitive process."

<<< **RTE** >>>

THE ABBREVIATION

As a short form of "route," there's "AAA suggestion," "GPS creation," "Hwy.," and "Numbered rd."

<<< **RYE** >>>

WHAT TO EAT

Rye is a delicatessen sandwich bread, an alternative to white or pumpernickel. It is an essential ingredient of a Reuben sandwich (with corned beef, Swiss cheese, and sauerkraut).

WHAT TO DRINK

Rye is also a type of whiskey, an essential ingredient of a Manhattan cocktail (with vermouth) and a highball (with club soda or ginger ale).

SLOE BERRIES ON A BLACKTHORN
HEDGE. (*FOTOLIA.COM*)

the

LETTER S

◀◀◀ SAC ▶▶▶

IN BIOLOGY

A sac is an anatomical bag or pouch.

THE ABBREVIATION

SAC, or Strategic Air Command, was a unit of the U.S. Air Force from 1946–1992.

◀◀◀ SAD ▶▶▶

THE ADJECTIVE

Commonly seen clues: "Downcast," "Feeling blue," "Melancholy," "Unfortunate," and "Woebegone."

◀◀◀ SADAT ▶▶▶

THE STATESMAN

Anwar Sadat was the president of Egypt from 1970 to 1981, preceded by Gamal Nasser and succeeded by Hosni Mubarak. Sadat shared the 1978 Nobel Peace Prize for his signing of the Camp David Accords.

◀◀◀ SAGE ▶▶▶

THE PERSON

Commonly seen noun clues in this sense: "Philosopher," "Pundit," and "Wise one." As an adjective, there's "Learned," "Prudent," and "Wise."

THE HERB

Sage is used in turkey stuffing, sausages, and meat marinades.

——— <<< **SAL** >>> ———

THE NAME

In real life, there's baseball players Bando and Maglie and actor Mineo. Sal Paradise is the narrator of Jack Kerouac's novel *On the Road*. Sal is the pizzeria owner portrayed by Danny Aiello in the Spike Lee film *Do the Right Thing*. There are two relevant old songs: "My Gal Sal," and "Fifteen Miles on the Erie Canal," which features a mule named Sal.

IN CHEMISTRY

"Sal" is a term for "salt" in chemical names such as sal soda (a.k.a. sodium carbonate).

——— <<< **SALE** >>> ———

THE NOUN

Commonly seen clues: "Ad headline," "Auction, for example," "Shopper's incentive," and "Store event."

——— <<< **SALSA** >>> ———

HOT TO HEAR

Salsa is a genre of lively Latin American music.

Not So Fast!

"Kitchen device": _ I C E R

The answer can be DICER or RICER.

HOT TO EAT

Salsa is also a sauce used for dipping with Tex-Mex foods such as burritos and nachos.

───── <<< **SAM** >>> ─────

REAL

Noted Sams include TV journalist Donaldson, statesman Houston, playwright Shepard, golfer Snead, retail mogul Walton, and actor Waterston.

FICTIONAL

There's the piano player in the film *Casablanca*, Tolkien character Sam Gamgee from *Lord of the Rings*, fictional sleuth Spade, Warner Bros. toon Yosemite Sam, and red, white, and blue Uncle Sam.

───── <<< **SAME** >>> ─────

THE ADJECTIVE

Commonly seen clues: "Ditto," "Identical," "Just the __," and "Unchanged."

───── <<< **SAN** >>> ─────

ON THE MAP

Most of the relevant place names are in California: San Clemente, San Diego, San Francisco, San Jose, San Mateo, and the San Andreas fault. The most notable exceptions: San Juan, Puerto Rico, and San Remo, Italy.

IN TOKYO

"San" is a Japanese term of respect, added as a suffix after a person's name or title.

──────── <<< **SANE** >>> ────────

THE ADJECTIVE

Commonly seen clues: "Levelheaded," "Lucid," "Rational," and "Sensible." Since mental health is a taboo subject for many crossword editors, you generally won't see clues like "Not batty."

──────── <<< **SANTA** >>> ────────

ON THE ROOF

In the yuletide sense, there's "Annual visitor," "North Pole resident," "Stocking stuffer," "Year-end temp," and clues referring to Santa's reindeer from the famous Clement Moore poem: Dancer, Dasher, Prancer, Vixen, Comet, Cupid, Donner, and Blitzen.

ON THE MAP

"Santa" cities include Santa Ana, Santa Clara, Santa Monica, and Santa Rosa in California, plus Santa Fe, New Mexico.

──────── <<< **SAO** >>> ────────

ON THE MAP

This Portuguese word for "saint" is clued most of the time by Brazil's largest city of São Paulo. There's also São Tomé and Principe (the island nation off the west coast of Africa), and São Miguel, the largest island of the Azores in the eastern Atlantic.

——— <<< **SAP** >>> ———

THE PERSON

Commonly seen clues in this sense: "Chump," "Dupe," "Easy mark," and "Patsy."

THE FLUID

From trees, there's "Maple product" and "Syrup source."

THE VERB

Commonly seen verb clues: "Drain," "Undermine," and "Weaken."

——— <<< **SARA** >>> ———

THE NAME

Famous Saras include Delano (mother of President Franklin Roosevelt), actress Gilbert, novelist Paretsky, poet Teasdale, and the Sara Lee brand of frozen foods.

——— <<< **SARI** >>> ———

WHAT TO WEAR

The sari is the traditional garment worn by Hindu women, especially in India. It is a long piece of fabric that is wrapped around the body.

——— <<< **SASE** >>> ———

THE ABBREVIATION

SASE is short for "self-addressed stamped envelope," often enclosed with a letter for the postpaid return of a manuscript (abbreviated "MS.") to an editor.

⟨⟨⟨ SASH ⟩⟩⟩

WHAT TO WEAR

A sash is a decorative band, belt, or scarf. Sashes are worn by Boy Scouts and Girl Scouts, beauty pageant contestants, military band marchers, and Japanese women (with a kimono, called an "obi").

WHAT NOT TO WEAR

A sash is the framework of a door or window, into which panes of glass are set.

⟨⟨⟨ SASS ⟩⟩⟩

THE NOUN/VERB

Commonly seen noun clues: "Backtalk," "Guff," and "Lip." As a verb, there's "Disrespect," "Get fresh with," and "Talk back to."

⟨⟨⟨ SAT ⟩⟩⟩

THE VERB

Commonly seen verb clues: "Convened," "Formed a lap," "Posed for a photo," "Rested," and "Took a chair."

THE ABBREVIATIONS

SAT may be short for the Scholastic Aptitude Test, taken by high-school seniors as a requirement for admission to college. It's also short for "Saturday."

⟨⟨⟨ SATE ⟩⟩⟩

THE VERB

To "sate" is to satisfy something fully, as one's appetite. It can also mean to fill to excess. Commonly seen clues in these senses include "Glut," "Gorge," "Overfill," and "Stuff."

◀◀◀ SCAM ▶▶▶

THE NOUN/VERB

Commonly seen noun clues: "Con game," "Fraud," and "Ripoff." As a verb, there's "Fleece" and "Hoodwink." Clues that work as both a noun and a verb: "Con," "Flimflam," "Hustle," and "Swindle."

◀◀◀ SCAN ▶▶▶

THE VERB

As a verb, "scan" has two opposite meanings: to examine hastily, or to examine with great care. It can also mean to read electronically, as a bar code at a checkout counter, or during a medical test such as a CAT scan.

◀◀◀ SCAR ▶▶▶

THE MARK

Commonly seen noun clues: "Duel mark," "Fight memento," and "Lasting impression." As a verb, there's "Mark permanently," and "Traumatize." Fictional wizard Harry Potter has a forehead scar in the shape of a lightning bolt.

THE NAME

Scar is the villainous lion in the Disney animated film *The Lion King*.

◀◀◀ SCAT ▶▶▶

THE EXCLAMATION

"Scat!" is commonly said to chase away people or animals.

THE MUSIC

Scat is a form of improvisational jazz singing using nonsense syllables instead of words. Noted scat singers include Ella Fitzgerald and Mel Tormé.

——— <<< **SCOT** >>> ———

THE NATIONALITY

Clues for SCOT usually refer to cities in Scotland (such as Aberdeen, Dundee, Edinburgh, and Glasgow) or natives of Scotland (such as poet Robert Burns, actor Sean Connery, and author Robert Louis Stevenson). There are also generic clues such as "Highlander" and "Kilt wearer."

——— <<< **SEA** >>> ———

LITERALLY

The world's seas include the Adriatic, Aegean, Baltic, Bering, Black, Caribbean, Caspian, and Red. The sea was the domain of the Greek god Poseidon and his Roman equivalent Neptune. There are also generic clues such as "Cruise locale" and "Ocean."

FIGURATIVELY

"Sea" can also mean a large quantity of anything.

——— <<< **SEAN** >>> ———

THE NAME

"Sean" is the Scottish equivalent of "John." Famous Seans include actor Astin, rap artist Combs, actor Connery, playwright O'Casey, and actor Penn.

<<< **SEAT** >>>

THE NOUN

In addition to a place to sit, a seat can be an elected office (such as a Senate seat), a government center (such as a county seat), or a membership in a stock exchange.

Need to Know: Mythical Gods

*The Greek gods that appear most often in crosswords
(with Roman equivalents in parentheses):*

APOLLO: god of music and poetry, son of Zeus and Leto, twin of Artemis

ARES (MARS): god of war, son of Zeus and Hera

EROS (CUPID, AMOR): god of love, son of Aphrodite

HADES (PLUTO): god of the underworld, son of Cronus and Rhea, brother of Zeus, Hera, and Poseidon

HERMES (MERCURY): messenger of the gods, son of Zeus and Maia

PAN: god of forests and pastures

ZEUS (JUPITER): supreme god, son of Cronus and Rhea, brother of Hades, Hera, and Poseidon: father of Ares, Apollo, Artemis, Athena, Hermes, and the Muses

The Norse gods that appear most often in crosswords:

LOKI: trickster god

ODIN: supreme god and god of war, husband of Frigg, father of Thor

THOR: god of thunder, son of Odin and Frigg

———— <<< **SEE** >>> ————

THE VERB

In the visual sense, there's "Look at," "Notice," "Observe," and "Spot." In the "comprehend" sense, there's "Catch on," "Get the point," and "Understand." In the "social" sense, there's "Date," "Drop in on," "Go out with," and "Visit." In the card game poker, to "see" a bet is to match the bet just made.

THE QUESTION

Colloquial phrases that clue the one-word sentence "See?" are similar to "Get it?" and "I told you so."

THE NOUN

A see is the jurisdiction of a bishop, a.k.a. "diocese."

———— <<< **SEED** >>> ————

THE NOUN

Plants and trees have seeds, and tennis tournaments have seeds (player rankings). Edible seeds include caraway, nutmeg, sesame, and sunflower. A seed may also be the beginning or source of anything, such as an idea.

THE VERB

"To seed" may mean to plant seeds, or to provide the initial capital for a startup business.

———— <<< **SEEP** >>> ————

THE VERB

Commonly seen clues: "Flow slowly," "Ooze," "Percolate," and "Trickle."

◀◀◀ SEER ▶▶▶

THE PERSON

Commonly seen clues: "Clairvoyant," "Crystal-ball user," "Fortune teller," "Soothsayer," and "Visionary."

◀◀◀ SEINE ▶▶▶

ON THE MAP

France's River Seine (pronounced "senn") flows through the cities of Paris and Rouen.

ON THE BOAT

A seine (pronounced "sane") is a type of fishing net. To "seine" is to fish with a seine.

◀◀◀ SELF ▶▶▶

THE NOUN

Commonly seen clues: "Ego," "Freudian subject," "Individual," and "Narcissist's love." It is the first "S" in "SASE" (self-addressed stamped envelope).

THE PREFIX

SELF- can be placed in front of many words, such as "evident," "help," "starter," and "worth."

THE MAG

Self is a women's magazine specializing in health, fitness, and nutrition.

Not So Fast!

"Type of tree": _ L D E R

The answer can be ALDER or ELDER.

<<< SELL >>>

THE VERB

Commonly seen clues: "Auction off," "Deal in," "Peddle," and "Unload." In Wall Street lingo, a bear is a pessimistic investor who is likely to place a sell order with a broker.

<<< SEMI >>>

THE NOUN

A "semi," short for "semitrailer," is a detachable trailer for hauling freight, to which a tractor is attached. Commonly seen clues in this sense: "18-wheeler," "Big rig," "Highway hauler," and "Teamster vehicle." It is also short for "semifinals," the next-to-last round of a tournament.

THE PREFIX

SEMI- (meaning "half") can be placed in front of many words, such as "circle," "conductor," "precious," and "private."

<<< SEN >>>

THE ABBREVIATION

As a short form for "Senator," there's "Capitol Hill VIP," "One of a D.C. 100," or any well-known senator's surname, followed by "for one: Abbr."

————— <<< **SENOR** >>> —————

IN SPAIN

"Señor" is the Spanish word for "mister."

————— <<< **SENSE** >>> —————

THE NOUN

Thinking "smart," there's "Brains," "Good judgment," and "Logical thinking." As used throughout this book, "sense" is also the meaning of a word in context. And don't forget the five senses (hearing, sight, smell, taste, and touch).

THE VERB

Commonly seen verb clues: "Detect," "Have a feeling," "Perceive," and "Pick up on."

————— <<< **SENT** >>> —————

THE VERB

Commonly seen clues in the literal sense: "Dispatched," "Mailed," "Shipped out," and "Transmitted." In a slangy sense, there's "Delighted," "Elated," and "Thrilled." Change any of these to the present tense, and you'll have the usual clues for "send," which appears in crosswords just a little less often than "sent."

————— <<< **SER** >>> —————

THE ABBREVIATION

As a short form of "sermon," there's "Rev.'s address" and "Sun. speech."

IN SPAIN

"*Ser*" is one of two Spanish verbs meaning "to be" (*estar* is the other).

⟫⟫ **SERA** ⟫⟫

THE NOUN

As the plural of "serum," commonly seen clues include "Antitoxins," "Blood fluids," and "Vaccines."

IN SPAIN

"*Sera*" is Spanish for "will be," as used in the title of the 1956 Doris Day tune "Que Sera, Sera."

IN ROME

"*Sera*" is the Italian word for "evening," as in the greeting "*Buona sera*" ("Good evening").

⟫⟫ **SERB** ⟫⟫

THE NATIVE

As a native of the Balkan nation of Serbia, clues will most often refer to the country's cities (such as Belgrade and Novi Sad), or its geographical neighbors (such as Bosnia, Bulgaria, Croatia, Macedonia, and Romania).

⟫⟫ **SERE** ⟫⟫

THE ADJECTIVE

Commonly seen clues include "Arid," "Bone-dry," "Parched," and "Withered."

───────<<< **SET** >>>───────

THE NOUN

A set can be a collection of anything, a part of a tennis match, where a movie shoot takes place, or the arrangement of hair as styled in a salon.

THE VERB

Commonly seen verb clues: "Arrange," "Determine," "Establish," "Harden," and "Prepare." The past tense of all these clues is often seen also, since the past tense of "set" is "set."

THE ADJECTIVE

"All in place," "Prepared," and "Ready" clue the adjective sense of "set."

───────<<< **SETA** >>>───────

BLANKETY-BLANKS

"__ good example" and "__ precedent" clue the phrase SET A.

THE NOUN

In biology, a seta is a stiff hair or bristle.

───────<<< **SEW** >>>───────

THE VERB

Commonly seen clues: "Baste," "Do darning," "Use a needle," and "Work as a tailor." Colloquially speaking, to "sew up" is to finalize, complete, or control exclusively.

———— <<< **SHA** >>> ————

THE SINGERS

The singing group Sha Na Na specializes in 1950s-era tunes.

———— <<< **SHE** >>> ————

THE PRONOUN

Women, ships, and half of the currently named hurricanes are called "she." And there's the "she" who "sells seashells by the seashore" in an old tongue twister.

BLANKETY–BLANKS

She Stoops to Conquer is a play by Oliver Goldsmith. Relevant colloquial phrases include "That's all she wrote" and the nautical "Steady as she goes" and "Thar she blows!"

———— <<< **SHEA** >>> ————

THE BALLPARK

Shea Stadium, in the New York City borough of Queens, was the home of the New York Mets from 1964 to 2008.

———— <<< **SHOT** >>> ————

THE NOUN

A shot can be a gun blast, a photograph, an opportunity or guess, a stroke or throw in sports, a hypodermic injection, or the quantity of liquor that fills a small glass.

THE VERB

As the past tense of "shoot," there's "Photographed" and "Took a picture of."

THE ADJECTIVE

Commonly seen adjective clues: "Exhausted," "Kaput," "Ruined," and "Worn out."

———— <<< **SILO** >>> ————

ON THE FARM

A silo is a cylindrical structure on a farm in which grain is stored.

ON THE BASE

A silo is also a military structure in which a ballistic missile (such as Minuteman or Titan) is stored.

———— <<< **SIR** >>> ————

HERE

Commonly seen "domestic" clues are "Military address" and "Polite title."

IN ENGLAND

"Sir" is the title given to a British man who has been knighted by the reigning monarch. Any well-known knighted Brit of past or present may be seen in a clue, such as actor Michael Caine, statesman Winston Churchill, actor Sean Connery, and scientist Isaac Newton.

Not So Fast!

"You, old-style": T H _ _

The answer can be THEE or THOU.

---⟪ **SIRE** ⟫---

TO A FARMER

A sire is the male parent of any four-legged animal, but most often clued in terms of horses. Synonyms of the verb form include "Beget" and "Father."

TO A ROYAL

"Sire" is a respectful term of address to a king or emperor.

---⟪ **SIS** ⟫---

THE RELATIVE

As a short form of "sister," commonly seen clues include "Bro's close relative," "Certain sibling," and "Family nickname."

THE EXCLAMATION

"Sis boom bah" is a common cheer at high school and college sports events.

---⟪ **SKI** ⟫---

THE VERB

Commonly seen verb clues: "Hit the slopes," "Schuss," "Slalom," "Travel on snow," and references to ski resorts (such as Aspen, Stowe, and Vail). The word is almost never defined in crosswords as the sporting-equipment noun.

---⟪ **SLAM** ⟫---

THE DOOR

In the "door" sense, there's "Close loudly" and "Shut forcefully."

THE DIS

In the sense of "criticize," there's "Castigate," "Criticize," and "Lambaste." SLAM may also be a noun in this sense, meaning "criticism."

IN BRIDGE

A slam is an achievement for a player in the card game.

 **SLAT**

THE NOUN

A slat is a narrow strip of wood or metal. Slats can be found in beds, benches, and Venetian blinds.

<<< **SLED** >>>

THE GLIDER

Sleds are pulled by dogs in Alaska, in the annual Iditarod race in particular. A sled named Rosebud is a key prop in the film *Citizen Kane*. Luges and toboggans are types of sleds used in the Winter Olympics.

<<< **SLIM** >>>

THE ADJECTIVE

In the "physique" sense, there's "Lanky," "Slender," "Svelte," and "Willowy." In the figurative sense, there's "Meager," "Negligible," and "Unlikely."

 **SLO**

TAKING IT EASY

The letters "SLO" are often seen on road pavement, as a warning for drivers to slow down. There's also the slo-mo (slow motion) replay on sports telecasts, and slo-pitch softball.

———<<< SLOE >>>———

THE FRUIT

The sloe is the plumlike fruit of the blackthorn tree. The liqueur sloe gin is flavored with it.

———<<< SLOT >>>———

THE NOUN

Things with slots include parking meters, piggy banks, and vending machines. Figuratively, a slot can be a place in a schedule or a job opening.

———<<< SLY >>>———

THE ADJECTIVE

Commonly seen clues: "Crafty," "Cunning," "Foxy," "Shrewd," "Sneaky," and "Wily."

———<<< SMEE >>>———

THE NAME

Smee is the villainous pirate associate of Captain Hook in James Barrie's *Peter Pan*.

———<<< SMELT >>>———

IN THE FOUNDRY

To "smelt" is to obtain metal from ore by melting.

IN THE WATER

A smelt is a small silvery fish commonly found in the Great Lakes.

―――――――― <<< **SNAG** >>> ――――――――

THE NOUN

Commonly seen clues: "Catch," "Complication," "Fly in the ointment," "Glitch," "Impediment," and "Sock woe." "Snag" is also a verb, but it's rarely clued that way in crosswords.

―――――――― <<< **SNAP** >>> ――――――――

THE NOUN

In the "simple" sense, there's "Breeze," "Cinch," and "Something easy." A snap can also be a clothes fastener, a ginger cookie, and one of the three sounds (snap, crackle, and pop) made by Rice Krispies cereal.

THE VERB

Commonly seen verb clues: "Break sharply," "Go ballistic," and "Flip out."

―――――――― <<< **SNEER** >>> ――――――――

THE LOOK

As a noun, there's "Scornful expression," "Sinister smile," and "Villainous glance." As a verb: "Curl the lip," "Scoff," and "Show disdain."

―――――――― <<< **SNIP** >>> ――――――――

THE VERB/NOUN

Commonly seen "action" clues: "Quick cut," "Salon sound," and

"Use scissors." A snip is also an insignificant or impertinent person.

<<< **SNIT** >>>

THE NOUN
Commonly seen clues: "Agitated state," "Huff," "Peeved mood," and "Tizzy."

<<< **SODA** >>>

THE DRINK
Commonly seen clues: "Carbonated beverage," "Fizzy drink," "Pop," and "Scotch partner."

<<< **SOHO** >>>

IN THE CITIES
Soho is the name of neighborhoods in the Manhattan borough of New York City and in London, England.

<<< **SOL** >>>

IN THE SKY
Sol is the astronomer's name for our sun.

IN THE SCALE
Sol (a.k.a. "so") is the fifth note of the musical scale, after fa and before la.

IN SPAIN
"Sol" is the Spanish word for "sun." The Costa del Sol ("sun coast") is a resort region of Spain on the Mediterranean.

─── <<< **SOLE** >>> ───

THE ADJECTIVE

Commonly seen adjective clues: "Exclusive," "Only," and "Unique."

THE NOUN

As a noun, a sole may be a food fish or the bottom of a shoe.

─── <<< **SOLO** >>> ───

HELPLESS

Commonly seen adverb clues: "By oneself," "Stag," and "Unaccompanied." As a noun, "Pilot's test" and "Recital piece." As a verb, "Fly alone" and "Perform an aria."

─── <<< **SON** >>> ───

ALL IN THE FAMILY

Commonly seen clues: "Heir, often," "Junior," "One of the Trinity," and "Young fellow." Also popular are references to well-known father-son pairs, such as Abel and Adam, Bob Cratchit and Tiny Tim, Kirk and Michael Douglas, and Homer and Bart Simpson.

Not So Fast!

"Genetic material": _ N A

The answer can be DNA or RNA.

─── <<< **SORE** >>> ───

THE ADJECTIVE

In the "angry" sense, there's "Miffed," "Peeved," "Steamed," and "Ticked off." In the "discomfort" sense, there's "Achy," "Painful," and "Tender."

─── <<< **SOS** >>> ───

AT SEA

As a maritime distress signal in Morse code, commonly seen clues include: "Call for help," "Coast Guard alert," "Mayday!," and "Sea plea."

AT THE SUPERMARKET

S.O.S. is a brand of steel-wool soap pads, whose best-known competitor is Brillo.

─── <<< **SOSO** >>> ───

NOT BAD

Commonly seen clues: "Fair," "Just O.K.," "Mediocre," and "Passable."

─── <<< **SPA** >>> ───

THE NOUN

A spa may be a mineral spring, a health resort with a spring, a fitness center, or a hot tub.

─── <<< **SPAN** >>> ───

THE NOUN/VERB

As a noun, there's "Bridge length," "Duration," "Period of time," and "Wing measurement." Commonly seen verb clues are variations of "Extend over" and "Reach across."

———— <<< **SPAR** >>> ————

IN A FIGHT

Commonly seen clues in this sense: "Exchange words," "Practice punching," "Train for a bout," and "Wrangle."

ON A SHIP

A spar is also a nautical pole that is used as a mast or boom to hold sails or handle cargo.

———— <<< **SPAT** >>> ————

CROSS WORDS

Commonly seen clues: "Disagreement," "Minor quarrel," "Petty argument," and "Tiff."

———— <<< **SPED** >>> ————

THE VERB

Commonly seen clues: "Exceeded the limit," "Rushed," "Stepped on it," and "Zoomed."

———— <<< **SPOT** >>> ————

THE VERB

Commonly seen verb clues: "Catch sight of," "Detect," and "Notice."

THE NOUN

A spot can be the location of something, a stain or mark, a place to park, or a predicament.

———— <<< **SRA** >>> ————

THE TITLE

Sra. is the abbreviation for *señora*, the Spanish word for "Mrs." The equivalent abbreviation in French is *Mme.*, short for *Madame.*

———— <<< **SRI** >>> ————

THE TITLE

In India, "sri" is a respectful title of address equivalent to Mr.

ON THE MAP

The island nation of Sri Lanka (formerly called Ceylon) is located in the Indian Ocean, southeast of India.

———— <<< **SRO** >>> ————

THE ABBREVIATION

SRO is short for "standing room only," often posted at a theater box office when all seats for that day's performance have been sold.

———— <<< **SRS** >>> ————

THE ABBREVIATION

"Srs." is short for "seniors." In crosswords, the seniors referred to are usually in school, with clues like "Grads-to-be: Abbr.," "SAT takers," and "Yearbook grp." Sometimes the reference is to senior citizens, with clues like "AARP members."

———— <<< **SSE** >>> ————

THE ABBREVIATION

SSE stands for the direction of south-southeast, which is the point opposite north-northwest (NNW) on a compass. You'll often see city clues like "Dallas-to-Houston dir.," where the second city is located south-southeast of the first. SSE and all the other compass points can be seen in weather reports (referring to wind direction) and on the screens of GPS devices.

———— <<< **SSR** >>> ————

THE ABBREVIATION

SSR stands for "Soviet Socialist Republic," a term for a constituent nation of the old Soviet Union, which went out of existence in 1991. Nations that were once SSRs include Armenia, Belarus, Kazakhstan, Estonia, Georgia, Latvia, Lithuania, and Ukraine.

———— <<< **SSS** >>> ————

THE ABBREVIATION

SSS stands for "Selective Service System," the federal agency that was once responsible for administering the military draft.

THE SOUND

SSS can also be clued as the sound of a tire leak, a radiator, a snake, or a barbecue.

―――――<<< **SST** >>>―――――

THE ABBREVIATION

SST stands for "supersonic transport," the class of passenger airplanes (no longer active) that flew faster than the speed of sound (a.k.a. Mach 1). The only SST to see regular passenger service was the Concorde, which was flown by Air France and British Airways between Europe and the United States.

―――――<<< **STA** >>>―――――

THE ABBREVIATION

"Sta." is short for "station." In crosswords, that's usually a train station, defined either with abbreviations such as R.R. (railroad) or B&O (Baltimore and Ohio railroad), or in reference to well-known railroad stations, such as Union Station (Washington, D.C.) and Penn Station (New York City).

―――――<<< **STAB** >>>―――――

THE NOUN

Noun clues are usually in the figurative sense, such as "Attempt," "Try," and "Wild guess."

THE VERB

Verb clues are always in the literal sense, such as "Pierce," "Puncture," and "Skewer."

―――――<<< **STAG** >>>―――――

THE PARTY

As a noun, a stag is a party attended by men only. By extension, it can also mean a male who attends a party unaccompanied by a woman.

THE BEAST

A stag is also a male deer, the mate of a doe.

⫷ STAIR ⫸

THE NOUN

Commonly seen clues are variations of "Flight component" and "Series of steps."

⫷ STAN ⫸

THE NAME

Famous Stans include satirist Freberg, jazz saxophonist Getz, film comedian Laurel (partner of Oliver Hardy), comic-book character creator Lee, baseball great Musial, and one of the juvenile characters in the animated sitcom *South Park*.

⫷ STAR ⫸

IN PERFORMANCE

As a noun, there's "Celebrity," "Headliner," and "Top banana." As a verb, "Get top billing," "Head the cast," and "Take the lead."

THE SHAPE

Things shaped like a star include a sheriff's badge, an asterisk, the symbol on the flag of Texas, and the stars awarded by film reviewers.

IN THE SKY

Commonly seen astronomical clues: "Constellation component,"

"Milky Way part," or references to well-known stars such as Antares, Polaris, and Rigel.

<<< STARE >>>

THE VERB
Commonly seen verb clues: "Gawk," "Gaze," and "Rubberneck."

THE NOUN
As a noun, the clue usually has two words, the second of which is "look," preceded by an apt adjective such as "Blank," "Impolite," or "Long."

<<< STAT >>>

THE NUMBER
As a short form of "statistic," clues may refer to statistics in baseball (such as RBIs and HRs), football (such as TDs), or economics (such as GNP).

THE ORDER
"Stat," when spoken by a physician, means "immediately," sort of the medical equivalent of "ASAP" or "PDQ."

<<< STATE >>>

ON THE MAP
Geographical clues may refer to any of the United States (specifically or generically, such as "Union member"), or sometimes the states of Australia (such as Queensland and New South Wales).

OFF THE MAP
As a noun, "state" means "condition"; as a verb it means "say." There's also the State Department of the U.S. government.

———— <<< **STAY** >>> ————

DON'T GO

Commonly seen verb clues: "Command to a canine," "Hang around," and "Remain." Clues for the related noun: "Hotel visit," "Legal delay," and "Postponement."

THE SUPPORT

A stay is a flat strip used for stiffening shirt collars and corsets.

———— <<< **STE** >>> ————

THE ABBREVIATION

"*Ste.*" is the short form of *sainte*, the French word for a female saint, Joan of Arc (Jeanne D'Arc in French) being the most notable. It is usually clued geographically, most often by the Michigan city of Sault Ste. Marie.

———— <<< **STEER** >>> ————

ON THE ROAD

Commonly seen clues in this sense: "Direct," "Navigate," and "Take the wheel."

ON THE RANCH

A steer is a type of bull that is raised for beef.

———— <<< **STEM** >>> ————

THE NOUN

Things with stems include flowers, mushrooms, pipes, wineglasses, and wristwatches.

Not So Fast!

"Pen point" or "Bird's beak": N _ B

In both senses, the answer can be NIB or NEB.

THE VERB

As a verb, "stem" can mean to stop or to dam up.

<<< **STEN** >>>

THE WEAPON

A Sten is a British submachine gun used during World War II.

THE NAME

Actress Anna Sten appeared in some 1930s films, including *Nana*.

<<< **STENO** >>>

ON THE JOB

A steno, short for "stenographer," takes dictation in shorthand, or takes down the proceedings in a courtroom.

<<< **STEP** >>>

THE NOUN

Commonly seen literal noun clues: "Dance move" and "Footfall." More figuratively, there's "Ladder rung," "Part of a plan," and "Short distance."

THE VERB

Commonly seen verb clues: "Stride" and "Walk."

———— <<< **STER** >>> ————

THE SUFFIX

-STER can be added at the end of many words, such as "gang," "poll," "pun," "quip," "tip," and "trick."

———— <<< **STET** >>> ————

ON A MANUSCRIPT

The word "stet" is written on a manuscript by an editor or proofreader, to indicate that certain text previously marked for deletion should be retained. It is the opposite of the editorial term "dele."

———— <<< **STEW** >>> ————

THE NOUN

Commonly seen culinary clues: "Crockpot creation," "Meat-and-potatoes dish," and references to particular types of stews, such as bouillabaisse, goulash, and hasenpfeffer.

THE VERB

Verb clues are usually in the figurative sense, such as "Fret," "Fume," and "Worry."

———— <<< **STIR** >>> ————

THE VERB

Commonly seen culinary clues: "Agitate," "Mix," and "Recipe direction." In the sense of "start to wake up," there's "Begin to awaken" and "Move slightly."

THE NOUN

As a synonym for "commotion," there's "Ado," "Fuss," "Hubbub," and "Tumult." As a slang term for a prison, there's "Hoosegow," "Poky," and "Slammer."

───── <<< **STLO** >>> ─────

ON THE MAP

The French town of St.-Lô, in the region of Normandy, was almost totally destroyed during the Allies' D-Day invasion of 1944.

───── <<< **STONE** >>> ─────

THE NOUN

A stone can be a rock (large or small), a precious gem, a fruit pit, or a British unit of weight equal to fourteen pounds.

THE NAME

Oliver Stone has directed such films as *JFK*, *Platoon*, and *Wall Street*.

───── <<< **STOP** >>> ─────

THE VERB

Commonly seen synonym clues: "Cease," "Discontinue," "Halt," and "Quit." In the imperative, there's "Cut that out!" and "Enough!"

THE NOUN

Buses and trains have stops, telegrams have "STOP"s (used to end sentences instead of periods), and church organs have stops, which admit air to their pipes.

<<< STORE >>>

THE NOUN

Commonly seen noun clues: "Boutique," "Mall tenant," and "Retail outlet."

THE VERB

As a verb, there's "Put away," "Save for later," and "Warehouse."

<<< STS >>>

THE ABBREVIATION

As a short form of "streets," there's "Ave. crossers," "GPS readings," and "Urban rds." As a short form of "saints," you'll see well-known saints given as examples, such as Mary, Paul, and Peter.

<<< STU >>>

THE NAME

Real people named Stu include actor Erwin and original Beatle Sutcliffe. There's also Disco Stu on the animated sitcom *The Simpsons*.

ALPHABETICALLY SPEAKING

Referring to the three consecutive letters, there's "Alphabetic trio" and "R-V connection."

<<< STY >>>

THE MESS

"On the farm" clues include "Hog's home," "Pigpen," and "Porker's place." Figuratively, a sty is any filthy place. While the word can also mean a type of eye irritation, it's almost never clued that way in crosswords.

———————<<< **SUE** >>>———————

THE VERB

Commonly seen verb clues: "Attorney's advice," "Seek damages from," and "Take to court."

THE NAME

The best-known Sue is mystery author Grafton. In song titles, there's "A Boy Named Sue" (Johnny Cash), "Peggy Sue" (Buddy Holly), and "Runaround Sue" (Dion).

THE T-BAR LIFT AT THE HEMSEDAL SKI
RESORT IN NORWAY. (*FOTOLIA.COM*)

the
LETTER
T

--------⫷⫷⫷ **TAB** ⫸⫸⫸--------

THE NOUN

In the "amount owed" sense, there's "Bar bill" and "Check." Tabs are also the projections on file folders, pull tabs are used to open soda cans, and don't forget about the Tab key on computer keyboards.

--------⫷⫷⫷ **TAD** ⫸⫸⫸--------

THE NOUN

Commonly seen clues: "Little bit," "Smidgen," and "Tiny amount."

THE NAME

Thomas "Tad" Lincoln was the youngest son of Abraham Lincoln.

--------⫷⫷⫷ **TAE** ⫸⫸⫸--------

THE INITIALS

The monogram of inventor Thomas Alva Edison, "The Wizard of Menlo Park," was T.A.E.

BLANKETY-BLANKS

Tae kwon do is a Korean martial art. Tae Bo is an aerobic exercise regimen.

--------⫷⫷⫷ **TAI** ⫸⫸⫸--------

BLANKETY-BLANKS

A mai tai is a type of rum cocktail. Tai chi is a Chinese martial art.

THE NAME

Tai Babilonia is an American former figure skater, the partner of Randy Gardner.

———————— <<< **TALC** >>> ————————

THE NOUN

Talc is a soft mineral used in making talcum powder.

———————— <<< **TALE** >>> ————————

THE NOUN

In the "story" sense, there's "Narrative," "Saga," and "Yarn." In the "untrue" sense, there's "Falsehood," "Lie," and "Whopper."

———————— <<< **TAN** >>> ————————

THE NOUN/VERB

Colors close to tan include almond, bronze, and caramel. Noun clues in the "beach" sense: "Basker's quest" and "Sunbather's goal." As a verb, there's "Catch some rays" and "Do leather work."

THE NAME

The books of novelist Amy Tan include *The Joy Luck Club* and *The Kitchen God's Wife*.

———————— <<< **TAPE** >>> ————————

THE NOUN

Commonly seen noun clues: "Package sealer," "Recording medium," "Sprinter's goal," and "VCR insert."

Not So Fast!

"Slow musical tempo": L _ _ _ O

The answer can be LENTO or LARGO.

THE VERB

Commonly seen verb clues: "Prerecord" and "Repair, as a sheet."

<<< **TAR** >>>

ON THE ROAD

Commonly seen clues in this sense: "Coal product," "Pavement goo," and "Roofing material."

ON THE OCEAN

"Tar" is an informal term for a sailor, with synonyms "Gob," "Salt," and "Sea dog."

<<< **TARA** >>>

THE PLACE

Tara is the Atlanta plantation that is the home of Scarlett O'Hara and her family in the Margaret Mitchell novel *Gone With the Wind*.

THE NAME

Tara Lipinski is a figure skater. Tara Reid is an actress.

——— <<< **TARO** >>> ———

THE EDIBLE

Taro is a tropical plant of the South Pacific islands, such as Hawaii and Tahiti. It is grown for its edible tuber, which is used to make the Polynesian food known as poi.

——— <<< **TART** >>> ———

THE ADJECTIVE

"Tart" can mean sour or sharp in the edible sense (with clues like "Lemony" and "Vinegary"), or in the sense of speaking (with clues like "Barbed," "Cutting," and "Snippy").

THE NOUN

As a noun, a tart is a small pie or pastry filled with fruit or jelly.

——— <<< **TBAR** >>> ———

ON THE MOUNTAIN

A T-bar is a type of lift used by skiers to reach the top of a slope.

——— <<< **TDS** >>> ———

IN FOOTBALL

As a short form of "touchdowns," commonly seen clues include: "NFL scores," "QB's successes" (QB is short for "quarterback"), and "Six-pt. plays."

——— <<< **TEA** >>> ———

THE DRINK

Commonly seen clues include "British beverage," "Coffee alternative," and "Herbal brew," plus references to tea varieties (such as

Earl Grey, oolong, and pekoe) and tea brands (such as Lipton and Tetley). A tea is an afternoon reception at which tea is served.

———— <<< **TEAR** >>> ————

THE VERB

As a verb, "tear" can mean to move quickly or to rip.

THE NOUNS

Pronounced "TEER," it's a drop from the eye. Pronounced "TARE," it's either a rip or a spree.

———— <<< **TEASE** >>> ————

JUST KIDDING

Commonly seen verb clues: "Make fun of," "Needle," "Taunt," and "Twit." As a noun, there's "Coquette" and "Flirt."

———— <<< **TED** >>> ————

THE NAME

Famous Teds include actor Danson, British poet Hughes, senator Kennedy, TV newsman Koppel, and media mogul Turner.

———— <<< **TEE** >>> ————

THE NOUN

A tee may be a collarless shirt, a small platform for a golf ball or football, the golf area where a ball is teed up, or a T-shaped pipe.

———— <<< **TEEM** >>> ————

THE VERB

Commonly seen clues: "Abound," "Overflow," "Rain hard," and "Swarm."

‹‹‹ TEEN ›››

THE PERSON

Commonly seen clues: "Adolescent," "High-schooler," and "New driver, often."

‹‹‹ TEL ›››

ON THE MAP

Tel Aviv is the second-largest city in Israel.

THE ABBREVIATION

As a short form for "telephone," there's "Addr. book entry," "Business card no.," and "Letterhead abbr."

‹‹‹ TELE ›››

THE PREFIX

TELE- can be added to many words, such as "cast," "conference," "graph," "marketing," "phone," and "vision." "Tele" is the T in TV and MTV, the music-video cable channel.

‹‹‹ TEN ›››

NUMERICALLY SPEAKING

Ten is a perfect score in gymnastics, the end of a knockout count in a boxing match, and the number of players on a lacrosse team. It's the lowest playing card in a royal flush. A portrait of Alexander Hamilton is on a $10 bill (a.k.a. sawbuck). The Roman numeral X is equivalent to 10.

‹‹‹ TENET ›››

THE NOUN

A tenet is a principle or doctrine of a group. Synonymous clues include "Belief," "Credo," and "Dogma."

———— <<< **TENSE** >>> ————

THE ADJECTIVE

Commonly seen adjective clues: "Edgy," "High-strung," "Nervous," and "Uptight."

THE NOUN

Verb tenses include past, present, future, and perfect.

———— <<< **TENT** >>> ————

THE NOUN

Commonly seen clues: "Camping gear," "Circus structure," "Loose-fitting dress," and "Portable shelter."

———— <<< **TERI** >>> ————

THE NAME

Actresses Garr, Hatcher, and Polo are the best-known people named Teri.

———— <<< **TESS** >>> ————

MRS. DICK TRACY

The lantern-jawed police detective in the Chester Gould comic strip wed Tess Truehart on Christmas Eve, 1949. She is portrayed by Glenne Headly in the 1990 film *Dick Tracy*, starring Warren Beatty.

THE "HARDY" GIRL

Tess Durbeyfield is the title character of the 1891 Thomas Hardy novel *Tess of the d'Urbervilles*. The 1979 film *Tess*, directed by Roman Polanski, is based on the Hardy novel; Nastassja Kinski has the title role.

OTHER TESSES, OTHER FILMS

Joanne Dru portrays Tess Millay, love interest of Montgomery Clift in the 1948 John Ford film *Red River*. Melanie Griffith portrays ambitious secretary Tess McGill in the 1988 film *Working Girl*. More recently, Julia Roberts is Tess Ocean, ex-wife of Danny Ocean (George Clooney), in the 2001 film *Ocean's Eleven* and its 2004 sequel *Ocean's Twelve*.

—————— <<< **TEST** >>> ——————

THE VERB/NOUN

Commonly seen noun clues: "Dry run," "Exam," "Midterm or final," and "Trial." As a verb, there's "Evaluate" and "Try out." Many of the clues for TEST work as both a noun and a verb, such as "Assay," "Audition," "Experiment," "Quiz," and "Sample."

—————— <<< **TET** >>> ——————

ON THE CALENDAR

In Vietnam, Tet is the New Year celebration.

—————— <<< **TETE** >>> ——————

IN FRANCE

"*Tête*" is the French word for "head," often clued humorously, such as "French bean?" and "Head of Paris?"

—————— <<< **THE** >>> ——————

THE ARTICLE

In English grammar, "the" is called the definite article (as opposed to "a" and "an," which are indefinite articles), which is usually ignored in alphabetization.

IN FRANCE

"*Thé*" is the French word for "tea," for which it may be clued as "*Café* alternative."

———— <<< **TIARA** >>> ————

THE NOUN

Commonly seen clues: "Beauty pageant headgear," "Papal wear," "Princess topper," and "Small crown."

———— <<< **TIE** >>> ————

WHAT TO WEAR (OR NOT)

Commonly seen clues in this sense: "Cravat," "Haberdashery buy," "Neckwear," and "Suit accessory." Figuratively, there's "Attachment" and "Connection."

THE NO-WIN SITUATION

In this sense, there's "Deadlock," "Overtime cause," "Stalemate," and "Standoff."

THE VERB

Verb clues may be related to either of the above senses, as in "Even the score" and "Make a knot."

Not So Fast!

"Family member": S I _

The answer can be SIB or SIS.

———<<< **TIER** >>>———

THE NOUN

Synonym clues include "Echelon," "Level," and "Rank." Stadiums, theaters, and wedding cakes may all have tiers.

———<<< **TILE** >>>———

IN THE HOUSE

A tile may be a piece of mosaic, linoleum, or ceramic, etc., found on the floor, wall, or ceiling of a home.

IN THE GAME

Games that use tiles include mah-jongg and Scrabble.

———<<< **TIM** >>>———

THE NAME

Famous Tims include actor Allen, director Burton, country singer McGraw, actor Robbins, and Tiny Tim from Dickens's *A Christmas Carol*.

———<<< **TIN** >>>———

THE NOUN

As the element (with chemical symbol Sn), commonly seen clues include "Pewter component," "Soft metal," "Tenth anniversary gift," and references to the countries that are major producers of tin, including Bolivia, Indonesia, and Malaysia. As a container, there's "Baking pan" and "Sardine holder."

———<<< **TINA** >>>———

THE NAME

The two best-known Tinas are actress Fey and singer Turner.

―――<<< **TIRE** >>>―――

THE VERB

Commonly seen verb clues: "Fatigue," "Grow weary," "Lose energy," and "Tucker out."

THE NOUN

As a noun, you'll see "Bicycle part," "Trunk item," and references to types of tires (such as spare and radial) and tire manufacturers (such as Bridgestone, Goodrich, Goodyear, and Michelin).

―――<<< **TIS** >>>―――

THE CONTRACTION

The poetic form of "it is," is usually clued either as part of the songs "Deck the Halls" ("'tis the season to be jolly") or "America" ("My country, 'tis of thee"), or as the title of the Frank McCourt memoir.

―――<<< **TMEN** >>>―――

THE COPS

T-men are federal investigative agents of the Treasury Department, a.k.a. "Feds." The Untouchables, led by Eliot Ness, were T-men. TMAN appears in crosswords somewhat less often than TMEN.

―――<<< **TNT** >>>―――

THE CHEMICAL

TNT, short for "trinitrotoluene," is used as an explosive.

ON THE TUBE

TNT, short for Turner Network Television, is a cable TV channel founded by Ted Turner.

◀◀◀ TOE ▶▶▶

ON YOUR FEET

In addition to feet, toes are parts of boots and shoes, and socks and stockings. Toes are the "little piggies" in the kids' nursery rhyme.

◀◀◀ TON ▶▶▶

THE MEASURE

As 2,000 pounds, commonly seen clues are variations of "Freight weight" and "Trucking unit." Figuratively speaking, a ton can also be a large quantity of anything.

◀◀◀ TONE ▶▶▶

THE NOUN/VERB

In the "hue" sense, there's "Coloring" and "Shade." In the "audible" sense, there's "Inflection," "Musical signal," "Pitch," and "Vocal quality." "Tone" can also refer to the resiliency of one's muscles, and as a verb, to improve those muscles.

◀◀◀ TONI ▶▶▶

THE NAME

The three best-known Tonis are singer Braxton, author Morrison, and singer Tennille.

◀◀◀ TOO ▶▶▶

THE ADVERB

In the "ditto" sense, there's "Also," "As well," "In addition," and "Moreover." In the "excessive" sense, there's "Overly" and "Unduly."

<<< TOR >>>

THE NOUN

A tor is a rocky pinnacle of a hill or mountain.

<<< TOT >>>

THE KID

Commonly seen "juvenile" clues: "Moppet," "Preschooler," "Rug-rat," and "Tyke."

THE VERB

To "tot up" means to calculate or to add.

<<< TOTE >>>

THE VERB/NOUN

Commonly seen verb clues: "Carry," "Lug," and "Schlep." As a noun, it's a bag with a handle.

<<< TRA >>>

IN MUSIC

"Tra" is sung as part of the filler syllables "tra-la-la."

Not So Fast!

"In the know": H _ P

The answer can be HIP or HEP.

———<<< **TRE** >>>———

IN ROME

"*Tre*" is the Italian word for "three," one more than *due* (Italian for "two").

———<<< **TREE** >>>———

LITERALLY SPEAKING

Commonly seen clues include "Arbor Day planting," "Fruit bearer," "Hammock holder," "Shade source," and references to many common types of trees, such as apple, maple, peach, sequoia, walnut, etc.

FIGURATIVELY SPEAKING

A tree is also a genealogy diagram and a device for preserving the shape of a shoe.

THE VERB

To "tree" someone or something is to corner them or put them in a difficult position.

———<<< **TRES** >>>———

IN FRANCE

"*Trés*" (pronounced "tray") is the French word for "very," seen in phrases like "*Trés bien!*" ("Very good!").

IN SPAIN

"*Tres*" (pronounced "trace") is the Spanish word for "three," one more than *dos* (two) and one less than *cuatro* (four).

—— ‹‹‹ TRI ››› ——

THE PREFIX

Meaning "three," TRI- can be added to words such as "angle" and "cycle." It is also what the first T stands for in TNT.

—— ‹‹‹ TRIO ››› ——

THE NOUN

A trio is any group of three persons or things, but is most commonly clued as a small group of musicians, either generically (such as "Quartet minus one" or "Small combo") or with specific examples (such as the singing groups the Dixie Chicks and the Supremes).

—— ‹‹‹ TROT ››› ——

THE NOUN/VERB

A trot is a slow running gait, applied to people or horses. Specifically for horses, it's also a harness race.

—— ‹‹‹ TRUE ››› ——

THE ADJECTIVE

Commonly seen clues: "Factual," "Faithful," "Loyal," and "Undeniable."

—— ‹‹‹ TSAR ››› ——

THE RULER

"Tsar" (also spelled "czar") was the title given to the emperors of Russia, mostly members of the Romanov dynasty. Alexander, Ivan the Terrible, Nicholas, and Peter the Great were all tsars.

◅◅◅ **TSE** ▻▻▻

IN CHINA

Mao Tse-tung (a.k.a. Mao Zedong) was the Communist leader of the People's Republic of China from 1949 into the 1970s. Lao-tse was an ancient Chinese philosopher.

THE INITIALS

TSE is the monogram of poet T. S. Eliot, whose works include *Ash Wednesday, The Waste Land,* "The Love Song of J. Alfred Prufrock," and a collection of light verse that was the basis for the Andrew Lloyd Webber musical *Cats.*

◅◅◅ **TWO** ▻▻▻

NUMERICALLY SPEAKING

Two is an early afternoon hour, and a "wee hour" in the a.m. In games, it's a playing card a.k.a. "deuce" and a dice role of "snake eyes." Two are needed to perform a duet, to ride on a seesaw, and (as the old saying goes) to tango.

UTE CHIEF SEVARA AND FAMILY, C. 1885. (DENVER PUBLIC LIBRARY)

the

LETTERS
U–Y

≪≪ UAR ≫≫

THE ABBREVIATION

The United Arab Republic was the former name of the combined nations of Egypt and Syria, from 1958 to 1961. Until 1971, Egypt alone was known as the United Arab Republic.

≪≪ UCLA ≫≫

THE ABBREVIATION

The University of California–Los Angeles is a member of the Pac-10 sports conference. Its teams are called the Bruins, whose rivals are the Trojans of U.S.C. Celebrities who attended UCLA include Arthur Ashe, Carol Burnett, and Jackie Robinson.

≪≪ ULNA ≫≫

THE BONE

The ulna is a bone in the human forearm, near the radius and the humerus.

≪≪ ULTRA ≫≫

THE PREFIX

ULTRA- can be added to words such as "sound" and "violet." It is the U in the UHF (ultrahigh frequency) television band.

THE NOUN

An ultra is an extremist, synonymous with "fanatic" and "revolutionary."

≪≪ UNDO ≫≫

THE VERB

Commonly seen clues: "Cancel," "Negate," "Nullify," "Take apart," and "Word processing command."

----- <<< **UNE** >>> -----

IN PARIS

"Une" is the French word for "one" (half of *deux*) or the article "a."

----- <<< **UNI** >>> -----

THE PREFIX

UNI- can be added to words such as "cycle," "form," "lateral," and "verse." Meaning "one," it is similar to "mono-."

----- <<< **UNIT** >>> -----

THE NOUN

Commonly seen clues: "Army group," "Condo division," "Curriculum section," and references to common units of measure such as the foot and the gallon.

----- <<< **UNITE** >>> -----

THE VERB

Commonly seen clues: "Bring together," "Fuse," "Join forces," and "Merge."

----- <<< **UNO** >>> -----

IN SPAIN

"Uno" is the Spanish word for "one." It's Italian for "one" too, but it's seldom clued that way.

THE GAME

Uno is a brand name for a card game.

───── <<< **UNTO** >>> ─────

THE PREPOSITION

The old-style preposition, frequently used in the Bible, is part of the Golden Rule ("Do unto others . . .").

───── <<< **UPON** >>> ─────

TWO WORDS

Commonly seen clues for UP ON include "Atop," "Familiar with," and "Versed in."

THE PREPOSITION

The preposition UPON is the second word of Edgar Allan Poe's "The Raven" ("Once upon a midnight dreary . . .") and many fairy tales ("Once upon a time . . . "). There's also Stratford-Upon-Avon, Shakespeare's hometown, and the colloquial "Upon my word!"

───── <<< **URAL** >>> ─────

ON THE MAP

Russia's Ural Mountains form part of the border between Europe and Asia. The Ural River originates in the Ural Mountains and flows into the Caspian Sea.

Not So Fast!

"Within: Prefix": E N _ O

The answer can be ENDO or ENTO.

◄◄◄ URGE ▶▶▶

THE VERB

Commonly seen verb clues: "Advocate," "Egg on," "Lobby for," and "Press."

THE NOUN

Commonly seen noun clues: "Craving," "Desire," "Hankering," and "Impulse."

◄◄◄ URIS ▶▶▶

THE NAME

The novels of author Leon Uris include *Battle Cry, Exodus, The Haj, Mila 18, Topaz,* and *Trinity.*

◄◄◄ URN ▶▶▶

THE CONTAINER

An urn may be a type of vase or a large machine that brews coffee or tea.

◄◄◄ USA ▶▶▶

ON THE MAP

In this sense, USA is usually defined either in terms of the treaties or organizations that it's a member of (such as NAFTA, NATO, and OAS), recent Olympic games it has hosted (1996 Summer and 2002 Winter), its geographic neighbors (Mexico and Canada), or the patriotic cheer for American teams at international athletic competitions.

ON TV

The USA cable network broadcasts much "second run" programming, plus the original series *Burn Notice, Monk,* and *Psych.*

<<< **USE** >>>

THE VERB

Commonly seen verb clues: "Consume," "Employ," "Put to work," and "Take advantage of."

THE NOUN

As a noun, there's "Application," "Function," "Purpose," and "Wear and tear."

<<< **USER** >>>

THE PERSON

"User" is most often defined as the user of a computer, with clues such as "__-friendly," "PC owner," "Software buyer," and "Web surfer."

<<< **USSR** >>>

ON THE MAP

Short for "Union of Soviet Socialist Republics" (a.k.a. the former Soviet Union), commonly seen clues include "Cold War letters," "Former U.N. member," and references to its onetime leaders (such as Lenin, Stalin, Khrushchev, and Gorbachev).

<<< **UTAH** >>>

ON THE MAP

UTAH is usually defined in terms of its cities (such as Provo and Salt Lake City), its neighboring states (Arizona, Colorado, Idaho, Nevada, and Wyoming, and with New Mexico at a single point at the "Four Corners" border), its National Parks (such as Bryce Canyon and Zion), or the Utah Jazz pro basketball team.

———— <<< **UTE** >>> ————

THE PEOPLE

The Utes are a Shoshonean Native American group now living primarily in Utah and Colorado. "Utes" is the nickname of the sports teams of the University of Utah at Salt Lake City.

ON THE ROAD

"Ute" is short for "utility" in the phrase "sport ute," another way to say "SUV."

———— <<< **VERA** >>> ————

THE NAME

The two best-known Veras are actress Miles and designer Wang.

THE PLANT

Aloe vera is a popular houseplant and a cosmetics additive.

———— <<< **YEAR** >>> ————

THE TIME

Commonly seen clues: "Calendar capacity," "Fiscal period," "Once around the sun," and "Wine label info."

——————— <<< **YES** >>> ———————

THE INTERJECTION

In this sense, the clue is usually a colloquial expression, such as "I do," "Of course!," "Okay!," and "You bet!"

THE VOTE

Commonly seen clues in this sense: "Affirmative response," "Assent," and "Thumbs-up vote."

ABOUT THE AUTHOR

Stanley Newman is one of America's best-known crossword professionals. He is currently a puzzle editor for the Long Island newspaper *Newsday,* the *Mind Stretchers* series for *Reader's Digest,* and a daily crossword with Web-search hints appearing on yahoo.com. Formerly the managing director of Random House's puzzles and games division, he is the author/editor of over 125 books, including the autobiography/instructional manual *Cruciverbalism,* the best-selling *Million Word Crossword Dictionary,* and *15,003 Answers: The Ultimate Trivia Encyclopedia.* He also conducts an annual Crossword University skill-building program on a luxury-liner cruise. Stan was the winner of the first U.S. Open Crossword Championship in 1982, and holds the world's record for the fastest completion of a *New York Times* crossword—2 minutes and 14 seconds.

Visit Stan's Crossword Land on the Web at www.StanXwords.com.